THE PRINCIPLES OF MASONIC LAW

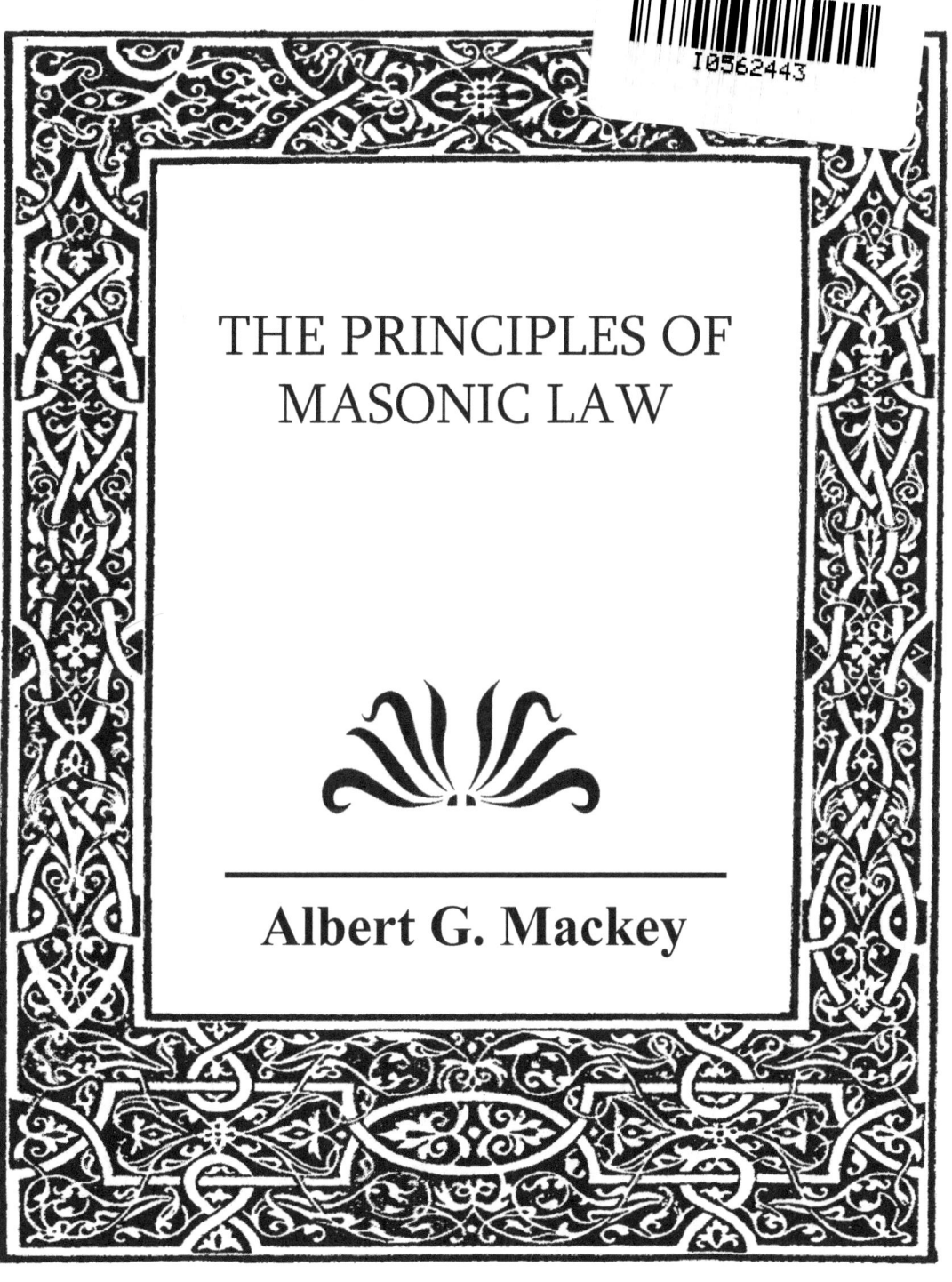

Albert G. Mackey

New York:
Jno. W. Leonard & Co., Masonic Publishers,
383 Broadway.

1856.

Contents

Contents

Contents

THE PRINCIPLES OF MASONIC LAW:

A Treatise on the Constitutional Laws,
Usages And Landmarks of Freemasonry,
By
Albert G. Mackey, M.D.,

Author of
"The Lexicon of Freemasonry," "The Mystic Tie," "Legends and
Traditions of Freemasonry," Etc., Etc.,

Grand Lecturer and Grand Secretary of The Grand Lodge of
South Carolina; Secretary General of the Supreme Council of the
Ancient and Accepted Rite for the Southern Jurisdiction of the
United States, Etc., Etc., Etc.

"Est enim unum jus, quo devincta est hominum societas, quod
lex constituit una; quae lex est recta ratio imperandi atque prohi-
bendi, quam qui ignorat is est injustus."

Cicero de Legibus. c. XV.

Preface.

IN presenting to the fraternity a work on the Principles of Masonic Law, it is due to those for whom it is intended, that something should be said of the design with which it has been written, and of the plan on which it has been composed. It is not pretended to present to the craft an encyclopedia of jurisprudence, in which every question that can possibly arise, in the transactions of a Lodge, is decided with an especial reference to its particular circumstances. Were the accomplishment of such an herculean task possible, except after years of intense and unremitting labor, the unwieldy size of the book produced, and the heterogeneous nature of its contents, so far from inviting, would rather tend to distract attention, and the object of communicating a knowledge of the Principles of Masonic Law, would be lost in the tedious collation of precedents, arranged without scientific system, and enunciated without explanation.

When I first contemplated the composition of a work on this subject, a distinguished friend and Brother, whose opinion I much respect, and with whose advice I am always anxious to comply, unless for the most satisfactory reasons, suggested the expediency of collecting the decisions of all Grand Masters, Grand Lodges, and other masonic authorities upon every subject of Masonic Law, and of presenting them, without commentary, to the fraternity.

But a brief examination of this method, led me to perceive that I would be thus constructing simply a digest of decrees, many of which would probably be the results of inexperience, of prejudice, or of erroneous views of the masonic system, and from which the authors themselves have, in repeated instances, subsequently receded--for Grand Masters and Grand Lodges, although entitled to great respect, are not infallible--and I could not, conscientiously, have consented to assist, without any qualifying remark, in the extension and perpetuation of edicts and opinions, which, however high the authority from which they emanated, I did not believe to be in accordance with the principles of Masonic jurisprudence.

Another inconvenience which would have attended the adoption of such a method is, that the decisions of different Grand Lodges and Grand Masters are sometimes entirely contradictory on the same points of Masonic Law. The decree of one jurisdiction, on any particular question, will often be found at variance with that of another, while a third will differ from both. The consultor of a work, embracing within its pages such distracting judgments, unexplained by commentary, would be in doubt as to which decision he should adopt, so that coming to the inspection with the desire of solving a legal question, he would be constrained to close the volume, in utter despair of extracting truth or information from so confused a mass of contradictions.

This plan I therefore at once abandoned. But knowing that

the jurisprudence of Masonry is founded, like all legal science, on abstract principles, which govern and control its entire system, I deemed it to be a better course to present these principles to my readers in an elementary and methodical treatise, and to develop from them those necessary deductions which reason and common sense would justify.

Hence it is that I have presumed to call this work "The Principles of Masonic Law." It is not a code of enactments, nor a collection of statutes, nor yet a digest of opinions; but simply an elementary treatise, intended to enable every one who consults it, with competent judgment, and ordinary intelligence, to trace for himself the bearings of the law upon any question which he seeks to investigate, and to form, for himself, a correct opinion upon the merits of any particular case.

Blackstone, whose method of teaching I have endeavored, although I confess "ab longo inter-vallo," to pursue, in speaking of what an academical expounder of the law should do, says:

"He should consider his course as a general map of the law, marking out the shape of the country, its connections, and boundaries, its greater divisions, and principal cities; it is not his business to describe minutely the subordinate limits, or to fix the longitude and latitude of every inconsiderable hamlet."

Such has been the rule that has governed me in the compilation of this work. But in delineating this "general map" of the Masonic Law, I have sought, if I may continue the metaphor, so to define boundaries, and to describe countries, as to give the inspector no difficulty in "locating" (to use an Americanism) any subordinate point. I have treated, it is true, of principles, but I have not altogether lost sight of cases.

There are certain fundamental laws of the Institution, concerning which there never has been any dispute, and which have come down to us with all the sanctions of antiquity, and universal acceptation. In announcing these, I have not always thought it necessary to defend their justice, or to assign a reason for their enactment.

The weight of unanimous authority has, in these instances, been deemed sufficient to entitle them to respect, and to obedience.

But on all other questions, where authority is divided, or where doubts of the correctness of my decision might arise, I have endeavored, by a course of argument as satisfactory as I could command, to assign a reason for my opinions, and to defend and enforce my views, by a reference to the general principles of jurisprudence, and the peculiar character of the masonic system. I ask, and should receive no deference to my own unsupported theories--as a man, I am, of course, fallible--and may often have decided erroneously. But I do claim for my arguments all the weight and influence of which they may be deemed worthy, after an attentive and unprejudiced examination. To those who may at first be ready--because I do not agree with all their preconceived opinions--to doubt or deny my conclusions, I would say, in the language of Themistocles, "Strike, but hear me."

Whatever may be the verdict passed upon my labors by my Brethren, I trust that some clemency will be extended to the errors into which I may have fallen, for the sake of the object which I have had in view: that, namely, of presenting to the Craft an elementary work, that might enable every Mason to know his rights, and to learn his duties.

The intention was, undoubtedly, a good one. How it has been executed, it is not for me, but for the masonic public to determine.

Albert G. Mackey.
Charleston, S.C., January 1st., 1856.

Introduction.
The Authorities for Masonic Law.

THE laws which govern the institution of Freemasonry are of two kinds, *unwritten and* written, and may in a manner be compared with the "lex non scripta," or common law, and the "lex seripta," or statute law of English and American jurists.

The "lex non scripta," or *unwritten law* of Freemasonry is derived from the traditions, usages and customs of the fraternity as they have existed from the remotest antiquity, and as they are universally admitted by the general consent of the members of the Order. In fact, we may apply to these unwritten laws of Masonry the definition given by Blackstone of the "leges non scriptae" of the English constitution--that "their original institution and authority are not set down in writing, as acts of parliament are, but they receive their binding power, and the force of laws, by long and immemorial usage and by their universal reception throughout the kingdom." When, in the course of this work, I refer to these unwritten laws as authority upon any point, I shall do so under the appropriate designation of "ancient usage."

The "lex scripta," or written law of Masonry, is derived from a variety of sources, and was framed at different periods. The following documents I deem of sufficient authority to substantiate any principle, or to determine any disputed question in masonic law.

1. The "Ancient Masonic charges, from a manuscript of the Lodge of Antiquity," and said to have been written in the reign of James II[1].

2. The regulations adopted at the General Assembly held in 1663, of which the Earl of St. Albans was Grand Master[2].

3. The interrogatories propounded to the Master of a lodge at the time of his installation, and which, from their universal adoption, without alteration, by the whole fraternity, are undoubtedly to be considered as a part of the fundamental law of Masonry.

4. "The Charges of a Freemason, extracted from the Ancient Records of Lodges beyond sea, and of those in England, Scotland, and Ireland, for the use of the Lodges in London," printed in the first edition of the Book of Constitutions, and to be found from p. 49 to p. 56 of that work[3].

5. The thirty-nine "General Regulations," adopted "at the annual assembly and feast held at Stationers' hall on St. John the

1   They will be found in Oliver's edition of Preston, p. 71, note, (U.M.L., vol. iii., p. 58), or in the American edition by Richards, Appendix i., note 5.

2   Found in Ol. Preston, n. 3 (p. 162. U.M.L., vol. iii., p. 134).

3   In all references to, or citations from, Anderson's Constitutions, I have used, unless otherwise stated, the first edition printed at London in 1723--a fac simile of which has recently been published by Bro. John W. Leonard, of New York. I have, however, in my possession the subsequent editions of 1738, 1755, and 1767, and have sometimes collated them together.

Baptist's day, 1721," and which were published in the first edition of the Book of Constitutions, p. 58 to p.

6. The subsequent regulations adopted at various annual communications by the Grand Lodge of England, up to the year 1769, and published in different editions of the Book of Constitutions. These, although not of such paramount importance and universal acceptation as the Old Charges and the Thirty-nine Regulations, are, nevertheless, of great value as the means of settling many disputed questions, by showing what was the law and usage of the fraternity at the times in which they were adopted.

Soon after the publication of the edition of 1769 of the Book of Constitutions, the Grand Lodges of America began to separate from their English parent and to organize independent jurisdictions. From that period, the regulations adopted by the Grand Lodge of England ceased to have any binding efficacy over the craft in this country, while the laws passed by the American Grand Lodges lost the character of general regulations, and were invested only with local authority in their several jurisdictions.

Before concluding this introductory section, it may be deemed necessary that something should be said of the "Ancient Landmarks of the Order," to which reference is so often made.

Various definitions have been given of the landmarks. Some suppose them to be constituted of all the rules and regulations which were in existence anterior to the revival of Masonry in 1717, and which were confirmed and adopted by the Grand Lodge of England at that time. Others, more stringent in their definition, restrict them to the modes of recognition in use among the fraternity. I am disposed to adopt a middle course, and to define the Landmarks of Masonry to be, all those usages and customs of the craft--whether ritual or legislative--whether they relate to forms and ceremonies, or to the organization of the society-- which have existed from time immemorial, and the alteration or abolition of which would materially affect the distinctive character of the institution or destroy its identity. Thus, for example, among the legislative landmarks, I would enumerate the office of Grand Master as the presiding officer over the craft, and among the ritual landmarks, the legend of the third degree. But the laws, enacted from time to time by Grand Lodges for their local government, no matter how old they may be, do not constitute landmarks, and may, at any time, be altered or expunged, since the 39th regulation declares expressly that "every annual Grand Lodge has an inherent power and authority to make new regulations or to alter these (viz., the thirty-nine articles) for the real benefit of this ancient fraternity, provided always that the old landmarks be carefully preserved."

Book First
The Law of Grand Lodges.

IT is proposed in this Book, first to present the reader with a brief historical sketch of the rise and progress of the system of Grand Lodges; and then to explain, in the subsequent sections, the mode in which such bodies are originally organized, who constitute their officers and members, and what are their acknowledged prerogatives.

Chapter I.
Historical Sketch.

Grand Lodges under their present organization, are, in respect to the antiquity of the Order, of a comparatively modern date. We hear of no such bodies in the earlier ages of the institution. Tradition informs us, that originally it was governed by the despotic authority of a few chiefs. At the building of the temple, we have reason to believe that King Solomon exercised an unlimited and irresponsible control over the craft, although a tradition (not, however, of undoubted authority) says that he was assisted in his government by the counsel of twelve superintendants, selected from the twelve tribes of Israel. But we know too little, from authentic materials, of the precise system adopted at that remote period, to enable us to make any historical deductions on the subject.

The first historical notice that we have of the formation of a supreme controlling body of the fraternity, is in the "Gothic Constitutions[4]" which assert that, in the year 287, St. Alban, the protomartyr of England, who was a zealous patron of the craft, obtained from Carausius, the British Emperor, "a charter for the Masons to hold a general council, and gave it the name of assembly." The record further states, that St. Alban attended the meeting and assisted in making Masons, giving them "good charges and regulations." We know not, however, whether this assembly ever met again; and if it did, for how many years it continued to exist. The subsequent history of Freemasonry is entirely silent on the subject.

The next general assemblage of the craft, of which the records of Freemasonry inform us, was that convened in 926, at the city of York, in England, by Prince Edwin, the brother of King Athelstane, and the grandson of Alfred the Great. This, we say, was the next general assemblage, because the Ashmole manuscript, which was destroyed at the revival of Freemasonry in 1717, is said to have stated that, at that time, the Prince obtained from his brother, the king, a permission for the craft "to hold

4   The Gothic Constitutions are that code of laws which was adopted by the General Assembly at York, in the year 926. They are no longer extant, but portions of them have been preserved by Anderson, Preston, and other writers.

a yearly communication and a general assembly." The fact that
such a power of meeting was then granted, is conclusive that it
did not before exist: and would seem to prove that the assemblies
of the craft, authorised by the charter of Carausius, had long since
ceased to be held. This yearly communication did not, however,
constitute, at least in the sense we now understand it, a Grand
Lodge. The name given to it was that of the "General Assembly of
Masons." It was not restricted, as now, to the Masters and Wardens of the subordinate lodges, acting in the capacity of delegates
or representatives, but was composed, as Preston has observed, of
as many of the fraternity at large as, being within a convenient
distance, could attend once or twice a year, under the auspices of
one general head, who was elected and installed at one of these
meetings, and who, for the time being, received homage as the
governor of the whole body. Any Brethren who were competent
to discharge the duty, were allowed, by the regulations of the
Order, to open and hold lodges at their discretion, at such times
and places as were most convenient to them, and without the necessity of what we now call a Warrant of Constitution, and then
and there to initiate members into the Order[5]. To the General
Assembly, however, all the craft, without distinction, were permitted to repair; each Mason present was entitled to take part in
the deliberations, and the rules and regulations enacted were the
result of the votes of the whole body. The General Assembly was,
in fact, precisely similar to those political congregations which,
in our modern phraseology, we term "mass meetings."

These annual mass meetings or General Assemblies contin-

---

5   Preston, book iv., sec, 2., p. 132, n. (U.M.L.,vol. iii., p. 109).

ued to be held, for many centuries after their first establishment, at the city of York, and were, during all that period, the supreme judicatory of the fraternity. There are frequent references to the annual assemblies of Freemasons in public documents. The preamble to an act passed in 1425, during the reign of Henry VI., just five centuries after the meeting at York, states that, "by the *yearly congregations and confederacies made by the Masons in their* general assemblies, the good course and effect of the statute of laborers were openly violated and broken." This act which forbade such meetings, was, however, never put in force; for an old record, quoted in the Book of Constitutions, speaks of the Brotherhood having frequented this "mutual assembly," in 1434, in the reign of the same king. We have another record of the General Assembly, which was held in York on the 27th December, 1561, when Queen Elizabeth, who was suspicious of their secrecy, sent an armed force to dissolve the meeting. A copy is still preserved of the regulations which were adopted by a similar assembly held in 1663, on the festival of St. John the Evangelist; and in these regulations it is declared that the private lodges shall give an account of all their acceptations made during the year to the General Assembly. Another regulation, however, adopted at the same time, still more explicitly acknowledges the existence of a General Assembly as the governing body of the fraternity. It is there provided, "that for the future, the said fraternity of Freemasons shall be regulated and governed by one Grand Master and as many Wardens as the said society shall think fit to appoint at every Annual General Assembly."

And thus the interests of the institution continued, until the beginning of the eighteenth century, or for nearly eight hundred years, to be entrusted to those General Assemblies of the fraternity, who, without distinction of rank or office, annually met at York to legislate for the government of the craft.

But in 1717, a new organization of the governing head was adopted, which gave birth to the establishment of a Grand Lodge, in the form in which these bodies now exist. So important a period in the history of Masonry demands our special attention.

After the death, in 1702, of King William, who was himself a Mason, and a great patron of the craft, the institution began to languish, the lodges decreased in number, and the General Assembly was entirely neglected for many years. A few old lodges continued, it is true, to meet regularly, but they consisted of only a few members.

At length, on the accession of George I., the Masons of London and its vicinity determined to revive the annual communications of the society. There were at that time only four lodges in the south of England, and the members of these, with several old Brethren, met in February, 1717, at the Apple Tree Tavern, in Charles street, Covent Garden, and organized by putting the oldest Master Mason, who was the Master of a lodge, in the chair; they then constituted themselves into what Anderson calls, "a Grand Lodge pro tempore;" resolved to hold the annual assembly and feast, and then to choose a Grand Master.

Accordingly, on the 24th of June, 1717, the assembly and feast were held; and the oldest Master of a lodge being in the chair, a list of candidates was presented, out of which Mr. Anthony Sayer was elected Grand Master, and Capt. Joseph Elliott and Mr. Jacob Lamball, Grand Wardens.

The Grand Master then commanded the Masters and Wardens of lodges to meet the Grand Officers every quarter, in communication, at the place he should appoint in his summons sent by the Tiler.

This was, then, undoubtedly, the commencement of that organization of the Masters and Wardens of lodges into a Grand Lodge, which has ever since continued to exist.

The fraternity at large, however, still continued to claim the right of being present at the annual assembly; and, in fact, at that meeting, their punctual attendance at the next annual assembly and feast was recommended.

At the same meeting, it was resolved "that the privilege of assembling as Masons, which had been hitherto unlimited, should be vested in certain lodges or assemblies of Masons convened in certain places; and that every lodge to be hereafter convened, except the four old lodges at this time existing, should be legally authorized to act by a warrant from the Grand Master for the time being, granted to certain individuals by petition, with the consent and approbation of the Grand Lodge in communication; and that, without such warrant, no lodge should be hereafter deemed regular or constitutional."

In consequence of this regulation, several new lodges received Warrants of Constitution, and their Masters and Wardens were ordered to attend the communications of the Grand Lodge. The Brethren at large vested all their privileges in the four old lodges, in trust that they would never suffer the old charges and landmarks to be infringed; and the old lodges, in return, agreed that the Masters and Wardens of every new lodge that might be constituted, should be permitted to share with them all the privileges of the Grand Lodge, except precedence of rank. The Brethren, says Preston, considered their further attendance at the meetings of the society unnecessary after these regulations were adopted; and therefore trusted implicitly to their Masters and Wardens for the government of the craft; and thenceforward the Grand Lodge has been composed of all the Masters and Wardens of the subordinate lodges which constitute the jurisdiction.

The ancient right of the craft, however, to take a part in the proceedings of the Grand Lodge or Annual Assembly, was fully acknowledged by a new regulation, adopted about the same time, in which it is declared that all alterations of the Constitutions must be proposed and agreed to, at the third quarterly communication preceding the annual feast, and be offered also to the perusal of *all* the Brethren before dinner, *even of the youngest Entered Apprentice*[6]

This regulation has, however, (I know not by what right,) become obsolete, and the Annual Assembly of Masons has long ceased to be held; the Grand Lodges having, since the beginning of the eighteenth century, assumed the form and organization which they still preserve, as strictly representative bodies.

Chapter II.
Of the Mode of Organizing Grand Lodges.

The topic to be discussed in this section is, the answer to the question, How shall a Grand Lodge be established in any state or country where such a body has not previously existed, but where there are subordinate lodges working under Warrants derived

---

6   General Regulations, art. xxxix.

from Grand Lodges in other states? In answering this question, it seems proper that I should advert to the course pursued by the original Grand Lodge of England, at its establishment in 1717, as from that body nearly all the Grand Lodges of the York rite now in existence derive their authority, either directly or indirectly, and the mode of its organization has, therefore, universally been admitted to have been regular and legitimate.

In the first place, it is essentially requisite that the active existence of subordinate lodges in a state should precede the formation of a Grand Lodge; for the former are the only legitimate sources of the latter. A mass meeting of Masons cannot assemble and organize a Grand Lodge. A certain number of lodges, holding legal warrants from a Grand Lodge or from different Grand Lodges, must meet by their representatives and proceed to the formation of a Grand Lodge. When that process has been accomplished, the subordinate lodges return the warrants, under which they had theretofore worked, to the Grand Lodges from which they had originally received them, and take new ones from the body which they have formed.

That a mass meeting of the fraternity of any state is incompetent to organize a Grand Lodge has been definitively settled--not only by general usage, but by the express action of the Grand Lodges of the United States which refused to recognize, in 1842, the Grand Lodge of Michigan which had been thus irregularly established in the preceding year. That unrecognized body was then dissolved by the Brethren of Michigan, who proceeded to establish four subordinate lodges under Warrants granted by the Grand Lodge of New York. These four lodges subsequently met in convention and organized the present Grand Lodge of Michigan in a regular manner.

It seems, however, to have been settled in the case of Vermont, that where a Grand Lodge has been dormant for many years, and all of its subordinates extinct, yet if any of the Grand Officers, last elected, survive and are present, they may revive the Grand Lodge and proceed constitutionally to the exercise of its prerogatives.

The next inquiry is, as to the number of lodges required to organize a new Grand Lodge. Dalcho says that *five* lodges are necessary; and in this opinion he is supported by the Ahiman Rezon of Pennsylvania, published in 1783 by William Smith, D.D., at that time the Grand Secretary of that jurisdiction, and also by some other authorities. But no such regulation is to be found in the Book of Constitutions, which is now admitted to contain the fundamental law of the institution. Indeed, its adoption would have been a condemnation of the legality of the Mother Grand Lodge of England, which was formed in 1717 by the union of only *four* lodges. The rule, however, is to be found in the Ahiman Rezon of Laurence Dermott, which was adopted by the "Grand Lodge of Ancient Freemasons," that seceded from the lawful Grand Lodge in 1738. But as that body was undoubtedly, under our present views of masonic law, schismatic and illegal, its regulations have never been considered by masonic writers as being possessed of any authority.

In the absence of any written law upon the subject, we are compelled to look to precedent for authority; and, although the Grand Lodges in the United States have seldom been established with a representation of less than four lodges, the fact that that of Texas was organized in 1837 by the representatives of only *three* lodges, and that the Grand Lodge thus instituted was at once recognized as legal and regular by all its sister Grand Lodges, seems to settle the question that three subordinates are sufficient to institute a Grand Lodge.

Three lodges, therefore, in any territory where a Grand Lodge does not already exist, may unite in convention and organize a Grand Lodge. It will then be necessary, that these lodges should surrender the warrants under which they had been previously working, and take out new warrants from the Grand Lodge which they have constituted; and, from that time forth, all masonic authority is vested in the Grand Lodge thus formed.

The Grand Lodge having been thus constituted, the next inquiries that suggest themselves are as to its members and its officers, each of which questions will occupy a distinct discussion.

Chapter III.
Of the Members of a Grand Lodge.

It is an indisputable fact that the "General Assembly" which met at York in 926 was composed of all the members of the fraternity who chose to repair to it; and it is equally certain that, at the first Grand Lodge, held in 1717, after the revival of Masonry, all the craft who were present exercised the right of membership in voting for Grand Officers[7], and must, therefore, have been considered members of the Grand Lodge. The right does

7   Chancellor Walworth, in his profound argument on the New York difficulties, asserted that this fact "does not distinctly appear, although it is, pretty evident that all voted."--p. 33. The language of Anderson does not, however, admit of a shadow of a doubt. "The Brethren," he says, "by a majority of hands, elected," &c.

not, however, appear to have been afterwards claimed. At this very assembly, the Grand Master who had been elected, summoned only the Master and Wardens of the lodges to meet him in the quarterly communications; and Preston distinctly states, that soon after, the Brethren of the four old lodges, which had constituted the Grand Lodge, considered their attendance on the future communications of the society unnecessary, and therefore concurred with the lodges which had been subsequently warranted in delegating the power of representation to their Masters and Wardens, "resting satisfied that no measure of importance would be adopted without their approbation."

Any doubts upon the subject were, however, soon put at rest by the enactment of a positive law. In 1721, thirty-nine articles for the future government of the craft were approved and confirmed, the twelfth of which was in the following words:

"The Grand Lodge consists of, and is formed by, the Masters and Wardens of all the regular particular lodges upon record, with the Grand Master at their head, and his Deputy on his left hand, and the Grand Wardens in their proper places."

From time to time, the number of these constituents of a Grand Lodge were increased by the extension of the qualifications for membership. Thus, in 1724, Past Grand Masters, and in 1725, Past Deputy Grand Masters, were admitted as members of the Grand Lodge. Finally it was decreed that the Grand Lodge should consist of the four present and all past grand officers; the Grand Treasurer, Secretary, and Sword-Bearer; the Master, Wardens, and nine assistants of the Grand Stewards' lodge, and the Masters and Wardens of all the regular lodges.

Past Masters were not at first admitted as members of the

Grand Lodge. There is no recognition of them in the old Constitutions. Walworth thinks it must have been after 1772 that they were introduced[8]. I have extended my researches to some years beyond that period, without any success in finding their recognition as members under the Constitution of England. It is true that, in 1772, Dermott prefixed a note to his edition of the Ahiman Rezon, in which he asserts that "Past Masters of warranted lodges on record are allowed this privilege (of membership) whilst they continue to be members of any regular lodge." And it is, doubtless, on this imperfect authority, that the Grand Lodges of America began at so early a period to admit their Past Masters to seats in the Grand Lodge. In the authorized Book of Constitutions, we find no such provision. Indeed, Preston records that in 1808, at the laying of the foundation-stone of the Covent Garden Theatre, by the Prince of Wales, as Grand Master, "the Grand Lodge was opened by Charles Marsh, Esq., attended by the *Masters and Wardens* of all the regular lodges;" and, throughout the description of the ceremonies, no notice is taken of Past Masters as forming any part of the Grand Lodge. The first notice that we have been enabled to obtain of Past Masters, as forming any part of the Grand Lodge of England, is in the "Articles of Union between the two Grand Lodges of England," adopted in 1813, which declare that the Grand Lodge shall consist of the Grand and Past Grand Officers, of the actual Masters and Wardens of all the warranted lodges, and of the "Past Masters of Lodges who have regularly served and passed the chair before the day of Union, and who continued,

---

8   Opinion of Chancellor Walworth upon the questions connected with the late masonic difficulties in the State of New York, p. 37. There is much historical learning displayed in this little pamphlet.

without secession, regular contributing members of a warranted lodge." But it is provided, that after the decease of all these ancient Past Masters, the representation of every lodge shall consist of its Master and Wardens, and one Past Master only. There is, I presume, no doubt that, from 1772, Past Masters had held a seat in the Athol Grand Lodge of Ancient Masons, and that they did not in the original Grand Lodge, is, I believe, a fact equally indisputable. By the present constitutions of the United Grand Lodge of England, Past Masters are members of the Grand Lodge, while they continue subscribing members of a private lodge. In some of the Grand Lodges of the United States, Past Masters have been permitted to retain their membership, while in others, they have been disfranchised.

On the whole, the result of this inquiry seems to be, that Past Masters have no inherent right, derived from the ancient landmarks, to a seat in the Grand Lodge; but as every Grand Lodge has the power, within certain limits, to make regulations for its own government, it may or may not admit them to membership, according to its own notion of expediency.

Some of the Grand Lodges have not only disfranchised Past Masters but Wardens also, and restricted membership only to acting Masters. This innovation has arisen from the fact that the payment of mileage and expenses to three representative would entail a heavy burden on the revenue of the Grand Lodge. The reason may have been imperative; but in the practice, pecuniary expediency has been made to override an ancient usage.

In determining, then, who are the constitutional members of a Grand Lodge, deriving their membership from inherent right, I should say that they are the Masters and Wardens of all regular lodges in the jurisdiction, with the Grand Officers chosen by them. All others, who by local regulations are made members, are so only by courtesy, and not by prescription or ancient law.

Chapter IV.
Of the Officers of a Grand Lodge.

The officers of a Grand Lodge may be divided into two classes, *essential and accidental*, or, as they are more usually called, *Grand and Subordinate*. The former of these classes are, as the name imports, essential to the composition of a Grand Lodge, and are to be found in every jurisdiction, having existed from the earliest times. They are the Grand and Deputy Grand Masters, the Grand Wardens, Grand Treasurer, and Grand Secretary. The Grand Chaplain is also enumerated among the Grand Officers, but the office is of comparatively modern date.

The subordinate officers of a Grand Lodge consist of the Deacons, Marshal, Pursuivant, or Sword-Bearer, Stewards, and others, whose titles and duties vary in different jurisdictions. I shall devote a separate section to the consideration of the duties of each and prerogatives of these officers.

Section I.
Of the Grand Master.

The office of Grand Master of Masons has existed from the very origin of the institution; for it has always been necessary that the fraternity should have a presiding head. There have been periods in the history of the institution when neither Deputies nor Grand Wardens are mentioned, but there is no time in its existence when it was without a Grand Master; and hence Preston, while speaking of that remote era in which the fraternity was governed by a General Assembly, says that this General Assembly or Grand Lodge "was not then restricted, as it is now understood to be, to the Masters and Wardens of private lodges, with the Grand Master and his Wardens at their head; it consisted of as many of the Fraternity *at large* as, being within a convenient distance, could attend, once or twice in a year, under the auspices of one general head, who was elected and installed at one of these meetings; and who for the time being received homage as the sole governor of the whole body.[9]" The office is one of great honour as well as power, and has generally been conferred upon some individual distinguished by an influential position in society; so that his rank and character might reflect credit upon the craft[10].

The Grand Mastership is an elective office, the election being annual and accompanied with impressive ceremonies of proclamation and homage made to him by the whole craft. Uniform usage, as well as the explicit declaration of the General Regulations[11], seems to require that he should be installed by the last Grand Master. But in his absence the Deputy or some Past Grand Master may exercise the functions of installation or investiture. In the organization of a new Grand Lodge, ancient precedent and

---

9   Preston, p. 131, n., Oliver's Edit. (U.M.L., vol. iii.,p. 109).
10   Of the thirty-six Grand Masters who have presided over the craft in England since the revival of Masonry in 1717, thirty have been noblemen, and three princes of the reigning family.
11   Article xxxiv.

the necessity of the thing will authorize the performance of the installation by the Master of the oldest lodge present, who, however, exercises, *pro hac vice*, the prerogatives and assumes the place of a Grand Master.

The Grand Master possesses a great variety of prerogatives, some of which are derived from the "lex non scripta," or ancient usage; and others from the written or statute law of Masonry[12].

I. He has the right to convene the Grand Lodge whenever he pleases, and to preside over its deliberation. In the decision of all questions by the Grand Lodge he is entitled to two votes. This is a privilege secured to him by Article XII. of the General Regulations.

It seems now to be settled, by ancient usage as well as the expressed opinion of the generality of Grand Lodges and of masonic writers, that there is no appeal from his decision. In June, 1849, the Grand Master of New York, Bro. Williard, declared an appeal to be out of order and refused to submit it to the Grand Lodge. The proceedings on that eventful occasion have been freely discussed by the Grand Lodges of the United States, and none of them have condemned the act of the Grand Master, while several have sustained it in express terms. "An appeal," say the Committee of Correspondence of Maryland, "from the decision of the Grand Master is an anomaly at war with every principle of Freemasonry, and as such, not for a moment to be tolerated or countenanced.[13]" This opinion is also sustained by the Committee of the Grand Lodge of Florida in the year 1851, and at various times by other Grand Lodges. On the other hand, several Grand Lodges have made de-

12   His most important prerogatives are inherent or derived from ancient usage.
13   Proceedings G.L. Maryland, 1849, p. 25.

cisions adverse to this prerogative, and the present regulations of the Grand Lodge of England seem, by a fair interpretation of their phraseology, to admit of an appeal from the Grand Master. Still the general opinion of the craft in this country appears to sustain the doctrine, that no appeal can be made from the decision of that officer. And this doctrine has derived much support in the way of analogy from the report adopted by the General Grand Chapter of the United States, declaring that no appeal could lie from the decision of the presiding officer of any Royal Arch body.

Since we have enunciated this doctrine as masonic law, the question next arises, in what manner shall the Grand Master be punished, should he abuse his great prerogative? The answer to this question admits of no doubt. It is to be found in a regulation, adopted in 1721, by the Grand Lodge of England, and is in these words:--"If the Grand Master should abuse his great power, and render himself unworthy of the obedience and submission of the Lodges, he shall be treated in a way and manner to be agreed upon in a new regulation." But the same series of regulations very explicitly prescribe, how this new regulation is to be made; namely, it is to be "proposed and agreed to at the third quarterly communication preceding the annual Grand Feast, and offered to the perusal of all the Brethren before dinner, in writing, even of the youngest entered apprentice; the approbation and consent of the majority of all the Brethren present being absolutely necessary, to make the same binding and obligatory.[14]" This mode of making a new regulation is explicitly and positively prescribed--it can be done in no other way--and those who accept the old regulations as the law of Masonry, must accept this provision with them. This

14   Art. xxxix.

will, in the present organization of many Grand Lodges, render it almost impracticable to make such a new regulation, in which case the Grand Master must remain exempt from other punishment for his misdeeds, than that which arises from his own conscience, and the loss of his Brethren's regard and esteem.

II. The power of granting dispensations is one of the most important prerogatives of the Grand Master. A dispensation may be defined to be an exemption from the observance of some law or the performance of some duty. In Masonry, no one has the authority to grant this exemption, except the Grand Master; and, although the exercise of it is limited within the observance of the ancient landmarks, the operation of the prerogative is still very extensive. The dispensing power may be exercised under the following circumstances:

1. The fourth old Regulation prescribes that "no lodge shall make more than five new Brothers at one and the same time without an urgent necessity.[15]" But of this necessity the Grand Master may judge, and, on good and sufficient reason being shown, he may grant a dispensation enabling any lodge to suspend this regulation and make more than five new Brothers.

2. The next regulation prescribes "that no one can be accepted a member of a particular lodge without previous notice, one month before given to the lodge, in order to make due inquiry into the reputation and capacity of the candidate." But here, also, it is held that, in a suitable case of emergency, the Grand Master may exercise his prerogative and dispense with this probation of one month, permitting the candidate to be made on the night of his application.

15   The word "time" has been interpreted to mean communication.

3. If a lodge should have omitted for any causes to elect its officers or any of them on the constitutional night of election, or if any officer so elected shall have died, been deposed or removed from the jurisdiction subsequent to his election, the Grand Master may issue a dispensation empowering the lodge to proceed to an election or to fill the vacancy at any other specified communication; but he cannot grant a dispensation to elect a new master in consequence of the death or removal of the old one, while the two Wardens or either of them remain--because the Wardens succeed by inherent right and in order of seniority to the vacant mastership. And, indeed, it is held that while one of the three officers remains, no election can be held, even by dispensation, to fill the other two places, though vacancies in them may have occurred by death or removal.

4. The Grand Master may grant a dispensation empowering a lodge to elect a Master from among the members on the floor; but this must be done only when every Past Master, Warden, and Past Warden of the lodge has refused to serve[16], because ordinarily a requisite qualification for the Mastership is, that the candidate shall, previously, have served in the office of Warden.

5. In the year 1723 a regulation was adopted, prescribing "that no Brother should belong to more than one lodge within the bills of mortality." Interpreting the last expression to mean three miles--which is now supposed to be the geographical limit of a lodge's jurisdiction, this regulation may still be considered as a part of the law of Masonry; but in some Grand Lodges, as that

---

16   And this is not because such past officer has an inherent right to the mastership, but because as long as such an one is present and willing to serve, there does not exist such an emergency as would authorize a dispensation of the law.

of South Carolina, for instance, the Grand Master will sometimes exercise his prerogative, and, dispensing with this regulation, permit a Brother to belong to two lodges, although they may be within three miles of each other.

6. But the most important power of the Grand Master connected with his dispensing prerogative is, that of constituting new lodges. It has already been remarked that, anciently, a warrant was not required for the formation of a lodge, but that a sufficient number of Masons, met together within a certain limit, were empowered, with the consent of the sheriff or chief magistrate of the place, to make Masons and practice the rites of Masonry, without such warrant of Constitution. But, in the year 1717, it was adopted as a regulation, that every lodge, to be thereafter convened, should be authorised to act by a warrant from the Grand Master for the time being, granted to certain persons by petition, with the consent and approbation of the Grand Lodge in communication. Ever since that time, no lodge has been considered as legally established, unless it has been constituted by the authority of the Grand Master. In the English Constitutions, the instrument thus empowering a lodge to meet, is called, when granted by the Grand Master, a Warrant of Constitution. It is granted by the Grand Master and not by the Grand Lodge. It appears to be a final instrument, notwithstanding the provision enacted in 1717, requiring the consent and approbation of the Grand Lodge; for in the Constitution of the United Grand Lodge of England, there is no allusion whatever to this consent and approbation.

But in this country, the process is somewhat different, and the Grand Master is deprived of a portion of his prerogative. Here, the instrument granted by the Grand Master is called a Dispensation.

The lodge receiving it is not admitted into the register of lodges, nor is it considered as possessing any of the rights and privileges of a lodge, except that of making Masons, until a Warrant of Constitution is granted by the Grand Lodge. The ancient prerogative of the Grand Master is, however, preserved in the fact, that after a lodge has been thus warranted by the Grand Lodge, the ceremony of constituting it, which embraces its consecration and the installation of its officers, can only be performed by the Grand Master in person, or by his special Deputy appointed for that purpose[17].

III. The third prerogative of the Grand Master is that of visitation. He has a right to visit any lodge within his jurisdiction at such times as he pleases, and when there to preside; and it is the duty of the Master to offer him the chair and his gavel, which the Grand Master may decline or accept at his pleasure. This prerogative admits of no question, as it is distinctly declared in the first of the Thirty-nine Regulations, adopted in 1721, in the following words:--

"The Grand Master or Deputy has full authority and right, not only to be present, but to preside in every lodge, with the Master of the lodge on his left hand, and to order his Grand Wardens to attend him, who are not to act as Wardens of particular lodges, but in his presence and at his command; for the Grand Master, while in a particular lodge, may command the Wardens of that lodge, or any other Master Masons, to act as his Wardens, *pro tempore*."

But in a subsequent regulation it was provided, that as the Grand Master cannot deprive the Grand Wardens of that office

---

17   What further concerns a lodge under dispensation is referred to a special chapter in a subsequent part of the work.

without the consent of the Grand Lodge, he should appoint no other persons to act as Wardens in his visitation to a private lodge, unless the Grand Wardens were absent. This whole regulation is still in existence.

The question has been lately mooted, whether, if the Grand Master declines to preside, he does not thereby place himself in the position of a private Brother, and become subject, as all the others present, to the control of the Worshipful Master. I answer, that of course he becomes subject to and must of necessity respect those rules of order and decorum which are obligatory on all good men and Masons; but that he cannot, by the exercise of an act of courtesy in declining to preside, divest himself of his prerogative, which, moreover, he may at any time during the evening assume, and demand the gavel. The Grand Master of Masons can, under no circumstances, become subject to the decrees and orders of the Master of a particular lodge.

IV. Another prerogative of the Grand Master is that of appointment; which, however, in this country, has been much diminished. According to the old regulations, and the custom is still continued in the Constitutions of the Grand Lodge of England, the Grand Master has the right of appointing his Deputy and Wardens. In the United States, the office has been shorn of this high prerogative, and these Officers are elected by the Grand Lodge. The Deputy, however, is still appointed by the Grand Master, in some of the States, as Massachusetts, North Carolina, Wisconsin, and Texas. The appointment of the principal subordinate officers, is also given to the Grand Master by the American Grand Lodges.

V. The last and most extraordinary power of the Grand Master, is that of *making Masons at sight*.

The power to "make Masons at sight" is a technical term, which may be defined to be the power to initiate, pass, and raise candidates by the Grand Master, in a lodge of emergency, or as it is called in the Book of Constitutions, "an occasional lodge," especially convened by him, and consisting of such Master Masons as he may call together for that purpose only--the lodge ceasing to exist as soon as the initiation, passing, or raising, has been accomplished and the Brethren have been dismissed by the Grand Master.

Whether such a power is vested in the Grand Master, is a question that, within the last few years, has been agitated with much warmth, by some of the Grand Lodges of this country; but I am not aware that, until very lately, the prerogative was ever disputed[18].

In the Book of Constitutions, however, several instances are furnished of the exercise of this right by various Grand Masters.

In 1731, Lord Lovel being Grand Master, he "formed an occasional lodge at Houghton Hall, Sir Robert Walpole's House in Norfolk," and there made the Duke of Lorraine, afterwards Emperor of Germany, and the Duke of Newcastle, Master Masons.[19]

I do not quote the case of the initiation, passing, and raising of Frederick, Prince of Wales, in 1737, which was done in "an occasional lodge," over which Dr. Desaguliers presided[20], because as Desaguliers was not the Grand Master, nor even, as has been in-

---

18   It is well known, although it cannot be quoted as authority, that the Athol Constitutions expressly acknowledged the existence of this prerogative. See Dermott's Ahiman Rezon.

19   Book of Constitutions, edit. 1767, p. 222.

20   Book of Const., p. 233.

correctly stated by the New York Committee of Correspondence, Deputy Grand Master, but only a Past Grand Master, it cannot be called *a making at sight*. He most probably acted under the dispensation of the Grand Master, who at that time was the Earl of Darnley.

But in 1766, Lord Blaney, who was then Grand Master, convened "an occasional lodge" and initiated, passed, and raised the Duke of Gloucester[21].

Again in 1767, John Salter, the Deputy, then acting as Grand Master, convened "an occasional lodge," and conferred the three degrees on the Duke of Cumberland[22].

In 1787, the Prince of Wales was made a Mason "at an occasional lodge, convened," says Preston, "for the purpose, at the Star and Garter, Pall Mall, over which the Duke of Cumberland, (Grand Master) presided in person.[23]"

But it is unnecessary to multiply instances of the right, exercised by former Grand Masters, of congregating occasional lodges, and making Masons at sight. It has been said, however, by the oppugners of this prerogative, that these "occasional lodges" were only special communications of the Grand Lodge, and the "makings" are thus supposed to have taken place under the authority of that body, and not of the Grand Master. The facts, however, do not sustain this position. Throughout the Book of Constitutions, other meetings, whether regular or special, are distinctly recorded as meetings of the Grand Lodge, while these "occasional lodges" appear only to have been convened by the Grand Master, for the

---

21   Book of Const., p. 313.
22   Book of Constitutions, p. 319.
23   Preston, p. 237, ed. 1802, (U.M.L., vol. iii., p. 223).

purpose of making Masons. Besides, in many instances, the lodge was held at a different place from that of the Grand Lodge, and the officers were not, with the exception of the Grand Master, the officers of the Grand Lodge. Thus the occasional lodge, which initiated the Duke of Lorraine, was held at the residence of Sir Robert Walpole, in Norfolk, while the Grand Lodge always met in London. In 1766, the Grand Lodge held its communications at the Crown and Anchor; but the occasional lodge, which, in the same year, conferred the degrees on the Duke of Gloucester, was convened at the Horn Tavern. In the following year, the lodge which initiated the Duke of Cumberland was convened at the Thatched House Tavern, the Grand Lodge continuing to meet at the Crown and Anchor.

This may be considered very conclusive evidence of the existence of the prerogative of the Grand Master, which we are now discussing, but the argument *a fortiori*, drawn from his dispensing power, will tend to confirm the doctrine.

No one doubts or denies the power of the Grand Master to constitute new lodges by dispensation. In 1741, the Grand Lodge of England forgot it for a moment, and adopted a new regulation, that no new lodge should be constituted until the consent of the Grand Lodge had been first obtained, "But this order, afterwards appearing," says the Book of Constitutions[24], "to be an infringement on the prerogative of the Grand Master, and to be attended with many inconveniences and with damage to the craft, was repealed."

It is, then, an undoubted prerogative of the Grand Master to constitute lodges by dispensation, and in these lodges, so consti-

24   Book of Constitutions, p. 247

tuted, Masons may be legally entered, passed, and raised. This is done every day. Seven Master Masons, applying to the Grand Master, he grants them a dispensation, under authority of which they proceed to open and hold a lodge, and to make Masons. This lodge is, however, admitted to be the mere creature of the Grand Master, for it is in his power, at any time, to revoke the dispensation he had granted, and thus to dissolve the lodge.

But, if the Grand Master has the power thus to enable others to confer the degrees and make Masons by his individual authority out of his presence, are we not permitted to argue *a fortiori* that he has also the right of congregating seven Brethren and causing a Mason, to be made in his sight? Can he delegate a power to others which he does not himself possess? And is his calling together "an occasional lodge," and making, with the assistance of the Brethren thus assembled, a Mason "at sight," that is to say, in his presence, anything more or less than the exercise of his dispensing power, for the establishment of a lodge under dispensation, for a temporary period, and for a special purpose. The purpose having been effected, and the Mason having been made, he revokes his dispensation, and the lodge is dismissed. If we assumed any other ground than this, we should be compelled to say, that though the Grand Master might authorise others to make Masons, when he was absent, as in the usual case of lodges under dispensation yet the instant that he attempted to convey the same powers to be exercised in his presence, and under his personal supervision, his authority would cease. This course of reasoning would necessarily lead to a contradiction in terms, if not to an actual absurdity.

It is proper to state, in conclusion, that the views here set forth are not entertained by the very able Committee of Foreign

Correspondence of the Grand Lodge of Florida, who only admit the power of the Grand Master to make Masons in the Grand Lodge. On the other hand, the Grand Lodge of Wisconsin, at its last communication, adopted a report, asserting "that the Grand Master has the right to make Masons at sight, in cases which he may deem proper"--and the Committee of Correspondence of New York declares, that "since the time when the memory of man runneth not to the contrary, Grand Masters have enjoyed the privilege of making Masons at sight, without any preliminaries, and at any suitable time or place."

The opinions of the two last quoted Grand Lodges embody the general sentiment of the Craft on this subject[25]. But although the prerogative is thus almost universally ceded to Grand Masters, there are many very reasonable doubts as to the expediency of its exercise, except under extraordinary circumstances of emergency.

In England, the practice has generally been confined to the making of Princes of the Royal Family, who, for reasons of state, were unwilling to reduce themselves to the level of ordinary candidates and receive their initiation publicly in a subordinate lodge.

But in the exercise of this prerogative, the Grand Master cannot dispense with any of the requisite forms of initiation, prescribed by the oral laws of the Order. He cannot communicate the degrees, but must adhere to all the established ceremonies-- the conferring of degrees by "communication" being a form un-

25   The existence of this prerogative is denied by the Grand Lodges of Missouri, Tennessee, Louisiana, and Massachusetts, while it is admitted by those of New York, Kentucky, North Carolina, South Carolina, Wisconsin, Vermont, Mississippi, Ohio, New Hampshire, Maryland, Indiana, Texas and Florida; in the last two, however, subject to limitation.

known to the York rite. He must be assisted by the number of Brethren necessary to open and hold a lodge. Due inquiry must be made into the candidate's character, (though the Grand Master may, as in a case of emergency, dispense with the usual probation of a month). He cannot interfere with the business of a regular lodge, by making one whom it had rejected, nor finishing one which it had commenced. Nor can he confer the three degrees, at one and the same communication. In short, he must, in making Masons at sight, conform to the ancient usages and landmarks of the Order.

Section II.
The Deputy Grand Master.

The office of Deputy Grand Master is one of great dignity, but not of much practical importance, except in case of the absence of the Grand Master, when he assumes all the prerogatives of that officer. Neither is the office, comparatively speaking, of a very ancient date. At the first reorganization of the Grand Lodge in 1717, and for two or three years afterwards, no Deputy was appointed, and it was not until 1721 that the Duke of Montagu conferred the dignity on Dr. Beal. Originally the Deputy was intended to relieve the Grand Master of all the burden and pressure of business, and the 36th of the Regulations, adopted in 1721, states that "a Deputy is said to have been always needful when the Grand Master was nobly born," because it was considered as a derogation from the dignity of a nobleman to enter upon the ordinary business of the craft. Hence we find, among the General Regulations, one which sets forth this principle in the following words:

"The Grand Master should not receive any private intimations of business, concerning Masons and Masonry, but from his Deputy first, except in such cases as his worship can easily judge of; and if the application to the Grand Master be irregular, his worship can order the Grand Wardens, or any other so applying, to wait upon the Deputy, who is immediately to prepare the business, and to lay it orderly before his worship."

The Deputy Grand Master exercises, in the absence of the Grand Master, all the prerogatives and performs all the duties of that officer. But he does so, not by virtue of any new office that he has acquired by such absence, but simply in the name of and as the representative of the Grand Master, from whom alone he derives all his authority. Such is the doctrine sustained in all the precedents recorded in the Book of Constitutions.

In the presence of the Grand Master, the office of Deputy is merely one of honour, without the necessity of performing any duties, and without the power of exercising any prerogatives.

There cannot be more than one Deputy Grand Master in a jurisdiction; so that the appointment of a greater number, as is the case in some of the States, is a manifest innovation on the ancient usages. District Deputy Grand Masters, which officers are also a modern invention of this country, seem to take the place in some degree of the Provincial Grand Masters of England, but they are not invested with the same prerogatives. The office is one of local origin, and its powers and duties are prescribed by the local regulations of the Grand Lodge which may have established it.

Section III.
Of the Grand Wardens.

The Senior and Junior Grand Wardens were originally appointed, like the Deputy, by the Grand Master, and are still so appointed in England; but in this country they are universally elected by the Grand Lodge. Their duties do not materially differ from those performed by the corresponding officers in a subordinate lodge. They accompany the Grand Master in his visitations, and assume the stations of the Wardens of the lodge visited.

According to the regulations of 1721, the Master of the oldest lodge present was directed to take the chair of the Grand Lodge in the absence of both the Grand Master and Deputy; but this was found to be an interference with the rights of the Grand Wardens, and it was therefore subsequently declared that, in the absence of the Grand Master and Deputy, the last former Grand Master or Deputy should preside. But if no Past Grand or Past Deputy Grand Master should be present, then the Senior Grand Warden was to fill the chair, and, in his absence, the Junior Grand Warden, and lastly, in absence of both these, then the oldest Freemason[26] who is the present Master of a lodge. In this country, however, most of the Grand Lodges have altered this regulation, and the Wardens succeed according to seniority to the chair of the absent Grand Master and Deputy, in preference to any Past Grand Officer.

---

26   That is, the one who has longest been a Freemason.

Section IV.
Of the Grand Treasurer.

The office of Grand Treasurer was first established in 1724, in consequence of a report of the Committee of Charity of the Grand Lodge of England. But no one was found to hold the trust until the 24th of June, 1727, when, at the request of the Grand Master, the appointment was accepted by Nathaniel Blackerby, Deputy Grand Master. The duties of the office do not at all differ from those of a corresponding one in every other society; but as the trust is an important one in a pecuniary view, it has generally been deemed prudent that it should only be committed to "a brother of good worldly substance," whose ample means would place him beyond the chances of temptation.

The office of Grand Treasurer has this peculiarity, that while all the other officers below the Grand Master were originally, and still are in England, appointed, that alone was always elective.

Section V.
Of the Grand Secretary.

This is one of the most important offices in the Grand Lodge, and should always be occupied by a Brother of intelligence and education, whose abilities may reflect honor on the institution of which he is the accredited public organ. The office was established in the year 1723, during the Grand Mastership of the Duke of Wharton, previous to which time the duties appear to have been discharged by the Grand Wardens.

The Grand Secretary not only records the proceedings of the Grand Lodge, but conducts its correspondence, and is the medium through whom all applications on masonic subjects are to be made to the Grand Master, or the Grand Lodge.

According to the regulations of the Grand Lodges of England, New York and South Carolina, the Grand Secretary may appoint an assistant, who is not, however, by virtue of such appointment, a member of the Grand Lodge. The same privilege is also extended in South Carolina to the Grand Treasurer.

Section VI.
Of the Grand Chaplain.

This is the last of the Grand Offices that was established, having been instituted on the 1st of May, in the year 1775. The duties are confined to the reading of prayers, and other sacred portions of the ritual, in consecrations, dedications, funeral services, etc. The office confers no masonic authority at all, except that of a seat and a vote in the Grand Lodge.

Section VII.
Of the Grand Deacons.

But little need be said of the Grand Deacons. Their duties correspond to those of the same officers in subordinate lodges. The office of the Deacons, even in a subordinate lodge, is of comparatively modern institution. Dr. Oliver remarks that they are not mentioned in any of the early Constitutions of Masonry, nor even

so late as 1797, when Stephen Jones wrote his "Masonic Miscel-
lanies," and he thinks it "satisfactorily proved that Deacons were
not considered necessary, in working the business of a lodge, before the very latter end of the eighteenth century.[27]"

But although the Deacons are not mentioned in the various
works published previous to that period, which are quoted by
Dr. Oliver, it is nevertheless certain that the office existed at a
time much earlier than that which he supposes. In a work in my
possession, and which is now lying before me, entitled "Every
Young Man's Companion, etc., by W. Gordon, Teacher of the
Mathematics," sixth edition printed at London, in 1777, there is a
section, extending from page 413 to page 426, which is dedicated
to the subject of Freemasonry and to a description of the working
of a subordinate lodge. Here the Senior and Junior Deacons are
enumerated among the officers, their exact positions described
and their duties detailed, differing in no respect from the expla-
nations of our own ritual at the present day. The positive testimony of this book must of course outweigh the negative testimony
of the authorities quoted by Oliver, and shows the existence in
England of Deacons in the year 1777 at least.

It is also certain that the office of Deacon claims an earlier
origin in America than the "very latter end of the eighteenth century;" and, as an evidence of this, it may be stated that, in the
"Ahiman Rezon" of Pennsylvania, published in 1783, the Grand
Deacons are named among the officers of the Grand Lodge, "as
particular assistants to the Grand Master and Senior Warden, in
conducting the business of the Lodge." They are to be found in
all Grand Lodges of the York Rite, and are usually appointed, the

27   Book of the Lodge, p. 115 (U.M.L., vol. i., book 2, p. 78).

Senior by the Grand Master, and the Junior by the Senior Grand
Warden.

Section VIII.
Of the Grand Marshal.

The *Grand Marshal*, as an officer of convenience, existed from
an early period. We find him mentioned in the procession of the
Grand Lodge, made in 1731, where he is described as carrying
"a truncheon, blue, tipped with gold," insignia which he still retains. He takes no part in the usual work of the Lodge; but his
duties are confined to the proclamation of the Grand Officers at
their installation, and to the arrangement and superintendence of
public processions.

The Grand Marshal is usually appointed by the Grand Master.

Section IX.
Of the Grand Stewards.

The first mention that is made of Stewards is in the Old Regulations, adopted in 1721. Previous to that time, the arrangements
of the Grand Feast were placed in the hands of the Grand Wardens; and it was to relieve them of this labor that the regulation
was adopted, authorizing the Grand Master, or his Deputy, to appoint a certain number of Stewards, who were to act in concert
with the Grand Wardens. In 1728, it was ordered that the number of Stewards to be appointed should be twelve. In 1731, a regulation was adopted, permitting the Grand Stewards to appoint

their successors. And, in 1735, the Grand Lodge ordered, that, "in consideration of their past service and future usefulness," they should be constituted a Lodge of Masters, to be called the Stewards' Lodge, which should have a registry in the Grand Lodge list, and exercise the privilege of sending twelve representatives. This was the origin of that body now known in the Constitutions of the Grand Lodges of England and New York[28], as the Grand Stewards' Lodge, although it has been very extensively modified in its organization. In New York, it is now no more than a Standing Committee of the Grand Lodge; and in England, although it is regularly constituted, as a Lodge of Master Masons, it is by a special regulation deprived of all power of entering, passing, or raising Masons. In other jurisdictions, the office of Grand Stewards is still preserved, but their functions are confined to their original purpose of preparing and superintending the Grand Feast.

The appointment of the Grand Stewards should be most appropriately vested in the Junior Grand Warden.

Section X.
Of the Grand Sword-Bearer.

Grand Sword-Bearer. --It was an ancient feudal custom, that all great dignitaries should have a sword of state borne before them, as the insignia of their dignity. This usage has to this day been preserved in the Masonic Institution, and the Grand Master's sword of state is still borne in all public processions by an officer specially appointed for that purpose. Some years after the reorganization of the Grand Lodge of England, the sword was borne

---

28   It was abolished in New York in 1854.

by the Master of the Lodge to which it belonged; but, in 1730, the Duke of Norfolk, being then Grand Master, presented to the Grand Lodge the sword of Gustavus Adolphus, King of Sweden, which had afterwards been used in war by Bernard, Duke of Saxe Weimar, and which the Grand Master directed should thereafter be adopted as his sword of state. In consequence of this donation, the office of Grand Sword-Bearer was instituted in the following year. The office is still retained; but some Grand Lodges have changed the name to that of *Grand Pursuivant*.

Section XI.
Of the Grand Tiler.

It is evident from the Constitutions of Masonry, as well as from the peculiar character of the institution, that the office of Grand Tiler must have existed from the very first organization of a Grand Lodge. As, from the nature of the duties that he has to perform, the Grand Tiler is necessarily excluded from partaking of the discussions, or witnessing the proceedings of the Grand Lodge, it has very generally been determined, from a principle of expediency, that he shall not be a member of the Grand Lodge during the term of his office.

The Grand Tiler is sometimes elected by the Grand Lodge, and sometimes appointed by the Grand Master.

Chapter V.
Of the Powers and Prerogatives
of a Grand Lodge.

Section I.
General View.

The necessary and usual officers of a Grand Lodge having been described, the rights, powers, and prerogatives of such a body is the next subject of our inquiry.

The foundation-stone, upon which the whole superstructure of masonic authority in the Grand Lodge is built, is to be found in that conditional clause annexed to the thirty-eight articles, adopted in 1721 by the Masons of England, and which is in these words:

"Every annual Grand Lodge has an inherent power and authority to make new regulations, or to alter these for the real benefit of this ancient fraternity; PROVIDED ALWAYS THAT THE OLD LANDMARKS BE CAREFULLY PRESERVED; and that such alterations and new regulations be proposed and agreed to at the third quarterly communication preceding the annual Grand Feast; and that they be offered also to the perusal of all the Brethren before dinner, in writing, even of the youngest Entered Apprentice: the approbation and consent of the majority of all the Brethren present being absolutely necessary, to make the same binding and obligatory."

The expression which is put in capitals--"provided always that the old landmarks be carefully preserved"--is the limiting clause which must be steadily borne in mind, whenever we attempt to enumerate the powers of a Grand Lodge. It must never be forgotten (in the words of another regulation, adopted in 1723, and incorporated in the ritual of installation), that "it is not in the power of any man, or body of men, to make any alteration or innovation in the body of Masonry."

"With these views to limit us, the powers of a Grand Lodge may be enumerated in the language which has been adopted in the modern constitutions of England, and which seem to us, after a careful comparison, to be as comprehensive and correct as any that we have been able to examine. This enumeration is in the following language:

"In the Grand Lodge, alone, resides the power of enacting laws and regulations for the permanent government of the craft, and of altering, repealing, and abrogating them, always taking care that the ancient landmarks of the order are preserved. The Grand Lodge has also the inherent power of investigating, regulating, and deciding all matters relative to the craft, or to particular lodges, or to individual Brothers, which it may exercise either of itself, or by such delegated authority, as in its wisdom and discretion it may appoint; but in the Grand Lodge alone resides the power of erasing lodges, and expelling Brethren from the craft, a power which it ought not to delegate to any subordinate authority in England."

In this enumeration we discover the existence of three distinct classes of powers:--1, a legislative power; 2, a judicial power; and 3, an executive power. Each of these will occupy a separate section.

Section II.
Of the Legislative Power of a Grand Lodge.

In the passage already quoted from the Constitutions of the Grand Lodge of England it is said, "in the Grand Lodge, alone, resides the power of enacting laws and regulations for the government of the craft, and of altering, repealing, and abrogating them." General regulations for the government of the whole craft throughout the world can no longer be enacted by a Grand Lodge. The multiplication of these bodies, since the year 1717, has so divided the supremacy that no regulation now enacted can have the force and authority of those adopted by the Grand Lodge of England in 1721, and which now constitute a part of the fundamental law of Masonry, and as such are unchangeable by any modern Grand Lodge.

Any Grand Lodge may, however, enact local laws for the direction of its own special affairs, and has also the prerogative of enacting the regulations which are to govern all its subordinates and the craft generally in its own jurisdiction. From this legislative power, which belongs exclusively to the Grand Lodge, it follows that no subordinate lodge can make any new bye-laws, nor alter its old ones, without the approval and confirmation of the Grand Lodge. Hence, the rules and regulations of every lodge are inoperative until they are submitted to and approved by the Grand Lodge. The confirmation of that body is the enacting clause; and, therefore, strictly speaking, it may be said that the subordinates only propose the bye-laws, and the Grand Lodge enacts them.

Section III.
Of the Judicial Power of a Grand Lodge.

The passage already quoted from the English Constitutions continues to say, that "the Grand Lodge has the inherent power of investigating, regulating and deciding all matters relative to the craft, or to particular lodges, or to individual Brothers, which it may exercise, either of itself, or by such delegated authority as in its wisdom and discretion it may appoint." Under the first clause of this section, the Grand Lodge is constituted as the Supreme Masonic Tribunal of its jurisdiction. But as it would be impossible for that body to investigate every masonic offense that occurs within its territorial limits, with that full and considerate attention that the principles of justice require, it has, under the latter clause of the section, delegated this duty, in general, to the subordinate lodges, who are to act as its committees, and to report the results of their inquiry for its final disposition. From this course of action has risen the erroneous opinion of some persons, that the jurisdiction of the Grand Lodge is only appellate in its character. Such is not the case. The Grand Lodge possesses an original jurisdiction over all causes occurring within its limits. It is only for expediency that it remits the examination of the merits of any case to a subordinate lodge as a *quasi* committee. It may, if it thinks proper, commence the investigation of any matter concerning either a lodge, or an individual brother within its own bosom, and whenever an appeal from the decision of a lodge is made, which, in reality, is only a dissent from the report of the lodge, the Grand Lodge does actually recommence the investigation *de novo*, and, taking the matter out of the lodge, to whom by its general usage it had been primarily referred, it places it in the hands of another committee of its own body for a new report. The course of action is, it is true, similar to that in law, of an appeal from an inferior to a superior tribunal. But the principle is different. The Grand Lodge simply confirms or rejects the report that has been made to it, and it may do that without any appeal having been entered. It may, in fact, dispense with the necessity of an investigation by and report from a subordinate lodge altogether, and undertake the trial itself from the very inception. But this, though a constitutional, is an unusual course. The subordinate lodge is the instrument which the Grand Lodge employs in considering the investigation. It may or it may not make use of the instrument, as it pleases.

Section IV.
Of the Executive Power of a Grand Lodge.

The English Constitutions conclude, in the passage that has formed the basis of our previous remarks, by asserting that "in the Grand Lodge, alone, resides the power of erasing lodges and expelling Brethren from the craft, a power which it ought not to delegate to any subordinate authority." The power of the Grand Lodge to erase lodges is accompanied with a coincident power of constituting new lodges. This power it originally shared with the Grand Master, and still does in England; but in this country the power of the Grand Lodge is paramount to that of the Grand Master. The latter can only constitute lodges temporarily, by dispensation, and his act must be confirmed, or may be annulled by the

Grand Lodge. It is not until a lodge has received its Warrant of Constitution from the Grand Lodge, that it can assume the rank and exercise the prerogatives of a regular and legal lodge.

The expelling power is one that is very properly intrusted to the Grand Lodge, which is the only tribunal that should impose a penalty affecting the relations of the punished party with the whole fraternity. Some of the lodges in this country have claimed the right to expel independently of the action of the Grand Lodge. But the claim is founded on an erroneous assumption of powers that have never existed, and which are not recognized by the ancient constitutions, nor the general usages of the fraternity. A subordinate lodge tries its delinquent member, under the provisions which have already been stated, and, according to the general usage of lodges in the United States, declares him expelled. But the sentence is of no force nor effect until it has been confirmed by the Grand Lodge, which may, or may not, give the required confirmation, and which, indeed, often refuses to do so, but actually reverses the sentence. It is apparent, from the views already expressed on the judicial powers of the Grand Lodge, that the sentence of expulsion uttered by the subordinate is to be taken in the sense of a recommendatory report, and that it is the confirmation and adoption of that report by the Grand Lodge that alone gives it vitality and effect.

The expelling power presumes, of course, coincidently, the reinstating power. As the Grand Lodge alone can expel, it also alone can reinstate.

These constitute the general powers and prerogatives of a Grand Lodge. Of course there are other local powers, assumed by various Grand Lodges, and differing in the several jurisdictions, but they are all derived from some one of the three classes that we have enumerated. From these views, it will appear that a Grand Lodge is the supreme legislative, judicial, and executive authority of the Masonic jurisdiction in which it is situated. It is, to use a feudal term, "the lord paramount" in Masonry. It is a representative body, in which, however, it constituents have delegated everything and reserved no rights to themselves. Its authority is almost unlimited, for it is restrained by but a single check:-- *It cannot alter or remove the ancient landmarks*.

Book Second
Laws of Subordinate Lodges.

Having thus succinctly treated of the law in relation to Grand Lodges, I come next in order to consider the law as it respects the organization, rights, powers, and privileges of subordinate Lodges; and the first question that will engage our attention will be, as to the proper method of organizing a Lodge.

Chapter I.
Of the Nature and Organization
of Subordinate Lodges.

The old charges define a Lodge to be "a place where Masons assemble and work;" and also "that assembly, or duly organized society of Masons." The lecture on the first degree gives a still more precise definition. It says that "a lodge is an assemblage of Masons, duly congregated, having the Holy Bible, square, and compasses, and a charter, or warrant of constitution, empowering them to work."

Every lodge of Masons requires for its proper organization, that it should have been congregated by the permission of some superior authority, which may be either a Grand Master or a Grand Lodge. When a lodge is organized by the authority of a Grand Master, it is said to work under a Dispensation, and when by the authority of a Grand Lodge, it is said to work under a warrant of constitution. In the history of a lodge, the former authority generally precedes the latter, the lodge usually working for some time under the dispensation of the Grand Master, before it is regularly warranted by the Grand Lodge. But this is not necessarily the case. A Grand Lodge will sometimes grant a warrant of constitution at once, without the previous exercise, on the part of the Grand Master, of his dispensing power. As it is, however, more usually the practice for the dispensation to precede the warrant of constitution, I shall explain the formation of a lodge according to that method.

Any number of Master Masons, not under seven, being desirous of uniting themselves into a lodge, apply by petition to the Grand Master for the necessary authority. This petition must set forth that they now are, or have been, members of a regularly constituted lodge, and must assign, as a reason for their application, that they desire to form the lodge "for the conveniency of their respective dwellings," or some other sufficient reason. The petition must also name the brethren whom they desire to act as their Master and Wardens, and the place where they intend to meet; and it must be recommended by the nearest lodge.

Dalcho says that not less than three Master Masons should sign the petition; but in this he differs from all the other authorities, which require not less than seven. This rule, too, seems to be founded in reason; for, as it requires seven Masons to constitute a quorum for opening and holding a lodge of Entered Apprentices, it would be absurd to authorize a smaller number to organize a lodge which, after its organization, could not be opened, nor make Masons in that degree.

Preston says that the petition must be recommended "by the Masters of three regular lodges adjacent to the place where the new lodge is to be held." Dalcho says it must be recommended "by three other known and approved Master Masons," but does not make any allusion to any adjacent lodge. The laws and regulations of the Grand Lodge of Scotland require the recommendation to be signed "by the Masters and officers of two of the nearest lodges." The Constitutions of the Grand Lodge of England require that it must be recommended "by the officers of some regular lodge." The recommendation of a neighboring lodge is the general usage of the craft, and is intended to certify to the superior authority, on the very best evidence that can be obtained, that, namely, of an adjacent lodge, that the new lodge will be productive of no injury to the Order.

If this petition be granted, the Grand Secretary prepares a document called a *dispensation*, which authorizes the officers named in the petition to open and hold a lodge, and to "enter, pass, and raise Freemasons." The duration of this dispensasation is generally expressed on its face to be, "until it shall be revoked by the Grand Master or the Grand Lodge, or until a warrant of constitution is granted by the Grand Lodge." Preston says, that the Brethren named in it are authorized "to assemble as Masons for forty days, and until such time as a warrant of constitution can be obtained by command of the Grand Lodge, or that authority be recalled." But generally, usage continues the dispensation only until the next meeting of the Grand Lodge, when it is either revoked, or a warrant of constitution granted.

If the dispensation be revoked by either the Grand Master or the Grand Lodge (for either has the power to do so), the lodge of course at once ceases to exist. Whatever funds or property it has accumulated revert, as in the case of all extinct lodges, to the Grand Lodge, which may be called the natural heir of its subordinates; but all the work done in the lodge, under the dispensation, is regular and legal, and all the Masons made by it are, in every sense of the term, "true and lawful Brethren."

Let it be supposed, however, that the dispensation is confirmed or approved by the Grand Lodge, and we thus arrive at another step in the history of the new lodge. At the next sitting of the Grand Lodge, after the dispensation has been issued by the Grand Master, he states that fact to the Grand Lodge, when, either at his request, or on motion of some Brother, the vote is taken on the question of constituting the new lodge, and, if a majority are in favor of it, the Grand Secretary is ordered to grant a warrant of constitution.

This instrument differs from a dispensation in many important particulars. It is signed by all the Grand Officers, and emanates from the Grand Lodge, while the dispensation emanates from the office of the Grand Master, and is signed by him alone. The authority of the dispensation is temporary, that of the warrant permanent; the one can be revoked at pleasure by the Grand Master, who granted it; the other only for cause shown, and by the Grand Lodge; the one bestows only a name, the other both a name and a number; the one confers only the power of holding a lodge and making Masons, the other not only confers these powers, but also those of installation and of succession in office. From these differences in the characters of the two documents, arise important differences in the powers and privileges of a lodge under dispensation and of one that has been regularly constituted. These differences shall hereafter be considered.

The warrant having been granted, there still remain certain forms and ceremonies to be observed, before the lodge can take its place among the legal and registered lodges of the jurisdiction in which it is situated. These are its consecration, its dedication, its constitution, and the installation of its officers. We shall not fully enter into a description of these various ceremonies, because they are laid down at length in all the Monitors, and are readily accessible to our readers. It will be sufficient if we barely allude to their character.

The ceremony of constitution is so called, because by it the lodge becomes constituted or established. Orthoepists define the verb to constitute, as signifying "to give a formal existence to anything." Hence, to constitute a lodge is to give it existence, character, and standing as such; and the instrument that warrants the person so constituting or establishing it, in this act, is very properly called the "warrant of constitution."

The consecration, dedication, and constitution of a lodge must be performed by the Grand Master in person; or, if he cannot conveniently attend, by some Past Master appointed by him as his special proxy or representative for that purpose. On the appointed evening, the Grand Master, accompanied by his Grand Officers, repairs to the place where the new lodge is to hold its meetings, the lodge[29] having been placed in the centre of the room and decently covered with a piece of white linen or satin. Having taken the chair, he examines the records of the lodge and the warrant of constitution; the officers who have been chosen are presented before him, when he inquires of the Brethren if they continue satisfied with the choice they have made. The ceremony of consecration is then performed. The Lodge is uncovered; and corn, wine, and oil--the masonic elements of consecration--are poured upon it, accompanied by appropriate prayers and invocations, and the lodge is finally declared to be consecrated to the honor and glory of God.

This ceremony of consecration has been handed down from the remotest antiquity. A consecrating--a separating from profane things, and making holy or devoting to sacred purposes--was practiced by both the Jews and the Pagans in relation to their temples, their altars, and all their sacred utensils. The tabernacle, as soon as it was completed, was consecrated to God by the unction of oil. Among the Pagan nations, the consecration of their temples was often performed with the most sumptuous offerings and ceremonies; but oil was, on all occasions, made use of as an element of the consecration. The lodge is, therefore, consecrated to denote that henceforth it is to be set apart as an asylum sacred to the cultivation of the great masonic principles of Friendship, Morality, and Brotherly Love. Thenceforth it becomes to the conscientious Mason a place worthy of his reverence; and he is tempted, as he passes over its threshold, to repeat the command given to Moses: "Put off thy shoes from off thy feet, for the place

---

29   This is a small chest or coffer, representing the ark of the covenant, and containing the three great lights of Masonry.

whereon thou standest is holy ground."

The corn, wine, and oil are appropriately adopted as the Masonic elements of consecration, because of the symbolic signification which they present to the mind of the Mason. They are enumerated by David as among the greatest blessings which we receive from the bounty of Divine Providence. They were annually offered by the ancients as the first fruits, in a thank-offering for the gifts of the earth; and as representatives of "the corn of nourishment, the wine of refreshment, and the oil of joy," they symbolically instruct the Mason that to the Grand Master of the Universe he is indebted for the "health, peace, and plenty" that he enjoys.

After the consecration of the lodge, follows its dedication. This is a simple ceremony, and principally consists in the pronunciation of a formula of words by which the lodge is declared to be dedicated to the holy Saints John, followed by an invocation that "every Brother may revere their character and imitate their virtues."

Masonic tradition tells us that our ancient Brethren dedicated their lodges to King Solomon, because he was their first Most Excellent Grand Master; but that modern Masons dedicate theirs to St. John the Baptist and St. John the Evangelist, because they were two eminent patrons of Masonry. A more appropriate selection of patrons to whom to dedicate the lodge, could not easily have been made; since St. John the Baptist, by announcing the approach of Christ, and by the mystical ablution to which he subjected his proselytes, and which was afterwards adopted in the ceremony of initiation into Christianity, might well be considered as the Grand Hierophant of the Church; while the mysterious and emblematic nature of the Apocalypse assimilated the mode of teaching adopted by St. John the Evangelist to that practiced by the fraternity. Our Jewish Brethren usually dedicate their lodges to King Solomon, thus retaining their ancient patron, although they thereby lose the benefit of that portion of the Lectures which refers to the "lines parallel." The Grand Lodge of England, at the union in 1813, agreed to dedicate to Solomon and Moses, applying the parallels to the framer of the tabernacle and the builder of the temple; but they have no warranty for this in ancient usage, and it is unfortunately not the only innovation on the ancient landmarks that that Grand Lodge has lately permitted.

The ceremony of dedication, like that of consecration, finds its archetype in the remotest antiquity. The Hebrews made no use of any new thing until they had first solemnly dedicated it. This ceremony was performed in relation even to private houses, as we may learn from the book of Deuteronomy[30]. The 30th Psalm is a song said to have been made by David on the dedication of the altar which he erected on the threshing-floor of Ornan the Jebusite, after the grievous plague which had nearly devastated the kingdom. Solomon, it will be recollected, dedicated the temple with solemn ceremonies, prayers, and thank-offerings. The ceremony of dedication is, indeed, alluded to in various portions of the Scriptures.

Selden[31] says that among the Jews sacred things were both dedicated and consecrated; but that profane things, such as private houses, etc., were simply dedicated, without consecration.

30　"What man is there that hath a new house and hath not dedicated it? Let him go and return to his house, lest he die in the battle and another man dedicate it." Deut. xx. 5.

31　De Syned. Vet. Ebraeor., 1. iii., c. xiv., Sec. 1.

The same writer informs us that the Pagans borrowed the custom of consecrating and dedicating their sacred edifices, altars, and images, from the Hebrews.

The Lodge having been thus consecrated to the solemn objects of Freemasonry, and dedicated to the patrons of the institution, it is at length prepared to be constituted. The ceremony of constitution is then performed by the Grand Master, who, rising from his seat, pronounces the following formulary of constitution:

"In the name of the most Worshipful Grand Lodge, I now constitute and form you, my beloved Brethren, into a regular lodge of Free and Accepted Masons. From this time forth, I empower you to meet as a regular lodge, constituted in conformity to the rites of our Order, and the charges of our ancient and honorable fraternity;--and may the Supreme Architect of the Universe prosper, direct, and counsel you, in all your doings."

This ceremony places the lodge among the registered lodges of the jurisdiction in which it is situated, and gives it a rank and standing and permanent existence that it did not have before. In one word, it has, by the consecration, dedication, and constitution, become what we technically term "a just and legally constituted lodge," and, as such, is entitled to certain rights and privileges, of which we shall hereafter speak. Still, however, although the lodge has been thus fully and completely organized, its officers have as yet no legal existence. To give them this, it is necessary that they be inducted into their respective offices, and each officer solemnly bound to the faithful performance of the duties he has undertaken to discharge. This constitutes the ceremony of installation. The Worshipful Master of the new lodge is required publicly to submit to the ancient charges; and then all,

except Past Masters, having retired, he is invested with the Past
Master's degree, and inducted into the oriental chair of King Solomon. The Brethren are then introduced, and due homage is paid
to their new Master, after which the other officers are obligated
to the faithful discharge of their respective trusts, invested with
their insignia of office, and receive the appropriate charge. This
ceremony must be repeated at every annual election and change
of officers.

The ancient rule was, that when the Grand Master and his
officers attended to constitute a new lodge, the Deputy Grand
Master invested the new Master, the Grand Wardens invested
the new Wardens, and the Grand Treasurer and Grand Secretary invested the Treasurer and Secretary. But this regulation has
become obsolete, and the whole installation and investiture are
now performed by the Grand Master. On the occasion of subsequent installations, the retiring Master installs his successor; and
the latter installs his subordinate officers.

The ceremony of installation is derived from the ancient
custom of inauguration, of which we find repeated instances in
the sacred as well as profane writings. Aaron was inaugurated,
or installed, by the unction of oil, and placing on him the vest-
ments of the High Priest; and every succeeding High Priest was
in like manner installed, before he was considered competent to
discharge the duties of his office. Among the Romans, augurs,
priests, kings, and, in the times of the republic, consuls were always inaugurated or installed. And hence, Cicero, who was an
augur, speaking of Hortensius, says, "it was he who installed me
as a member of the college of augurs, so that I was bound by the

constitution of the order to respect and honour him as a parent.[32]"
The object and intention of the ancient inauguration and the Masonic installation are precisely the same, namely, that of setting apart and consecrating a person to the duties of a certain office.

The ceremonies, thus briefly described, were not always necessary to legalize a congregation of Masons. Until the year 1717, the custom of confining the privileges of Masonry, by a warrant of constitution, to certain individuals, was wholly unknown. Previous to that time, a requisite number of Master Masons were authorized by the ancient charges to congregate together, temporarily, at their own discretion, and as best suited their convenience, and then and there to open and hold lodges and make Masons; making, however, their return, and paying their tribute to the General Assembly, to which all the fraternity annually repaired, and by whose awards the craft were governed.

Preston, speaking of this ancient privilege, says: "A sufficient number of Masons met together within a certain district, with the consent of the sheriff or chief magistrate of the place, were empowered at this time to make Masons and practice the rights of Masonry, without a warrant of constitution." This privilege, Preston says, was inherent in them as individuals, and continued to be enjoyed by the old lodges, which formed the Grand Lodge in 1717, as long as they were in existence.

But on the 24th June, 1717, the Grand Lodge of England adopted the following regulation: "That the privilege of assembling as Masons, which had hitherto been unlimited, should be vested in certain lodges or assemblies of Masons, convened in certain places; and that every lodge to be hereafter convened, except the

32   Cicero, Brut. i.

four old lodges at this time existing, should be legally authorized to act by a warrant from the Grand Master for the time being, granted to certain individuals by petition, with the consent and approbation of the Grand Lodge in communication; and that, without such warrant, no lodge should be hereafter deemed regular or constitutional."

This regulation has ever since continued in force, and it is the original law under which warrants of constitution are now granted by Grand Lodges for the organization of their subordinates.

Chapter II.
Of Lodges under Dispensation.

It is evident, from what has already been said, that there are two kinds of lodges, each regular in itself, but each peculiar and distinct in its character. There are lodges working under a dispensation, and lodges working under a warrant of constitution. Each of these will require a separate consideration. The former will be the subject of the present chapter.

A lodge working under a dispensation is a merely temporary body, originated for a special purpose, and is therefore possessed of very circumscribed powers. The dispensation, or authority under which it acts, expressly specifies that the persons to whom it is given are allowed to congregate that they may "admit, enter, pass, and raise Freemasons;" no other powers are conferred either by words or implication, and, indeed, sometimes the dispensation states, that that congregation is to be "with the sole intent and view, that the Brethren so congregated, admitted, entered, and made, when they become a sufficient number, may be duly warranted and constituted for being and holding a regular lodge.[33"]

A lodge under dispensation is simply the creature of the Grand Master. To him it is indebted for its existence, and on his will depends the duration of that existence. He may at any time revoke the dispensation, and the dissolution of the lodge would be the instant result. Hence a lodge working under a dispensation can scarcely, with strict technical propriety, be called a lodge; it is, more properly speaking, a congregation of Masons, acting as the proxy of the Grand Master.

With these views of the origin and character of lodges under dispensation, we will be better prepared to understand the nature and extent of the powers which they possess.

A lodge under dispensation can make no bye-laws. It is governed, during its temporary existence, by the general Constitutions of the Order and the rules and regulations of the Grand Lodge in whose jurisdiction it is situated. In fact, as the bye-laws of no lodge are operative until they are confirmed by the Grand Lodge, and as a lodge working under a dispensation ceases to exist as such as soon as the Grand Lodge meets, it is evident that it would be absurd to frame a code of laws which would have no efficacy, for want of proper confirmation, and which, when the time and opportunity for confirmation had arrived, would be needless, as the society for which they were framed would then have no legal existence--a new body (the warranted lodge) having taken its place.

A lodge under dispensation cannot elect officers. The Master

---

33   See such a form of Dispensation in Cole's Masonic Library, p. 91.

and Wardens are nominated by the Brethren, and, if this nomination is approved, they are appointed by the Grand Master. In giving them permission to meet and make Masons, he gave them no power to do anything else. A dispensation is itself a setting aside of the law, and an exception to a general principle; it must, therefore, be construed literally. What is not granted in express terms, is not granted at all. And, therefore, as nothing is said of the election of officers, no such election can be held. The Master may, however, and always does for convenience, appoint a competent Brother to keep a record of the proceedings; but this is a temporary appointment, at the pleasure of the Master, whose deputy or assistant he is; for the Grand Lodge looks only to the Master for the records, and the office is not legally recognized. In like manner, he may depute a trusty Brother to take charge of the funds, and must, of course, from time to time, appoint the deacons and tiler for the necessary working of the lodge.

As there can be no election, neither can there be any installation, which, of course, always presumes a previous election for a determinate period. Besides, the installation of officers is a part of the ceremony of constitution, and therefore not even the Master and Wardens of a lodge under dispensation are entitled to be thus solemnly inducted into office.

A lodge under dispensation can elect no members. The Master and Wardens, who are named in the dispensation, are, in point of fact, the only persons recognized as constituting the lodge. To them is granted the privilege, as proxies of the Grand Master, of making Masons; and for this purpose they are authorized to congregate a sufficient number of Brethren to assist them in the ceremonies. But neither the Master and Wardens, nor the Brethren, thus congregated have received any power of electing members. Nor are the persons made in a lodge under dispensation, to be considered as members of the lodge; for, as has already been shown, they have none of the rights and privileges which attach to membership--they can neither make bye-laws nor elect officers. They, however, become members of the lodge as soon as it receives its warrant of constitution.

Chapter III.
Of Lodges Working under a
Warrant of Constitution.

Section I.
Of the Powers and Rights of a Lodge.

In respect to the powers and privileges possessed by a lodge working under a warrant of constitution, we may say, as a general principle, that whatever it does possess is inherent in it--nothing has been delegated by either the Grand Master or the Grand Lodge--but that all its rights and powers are derived originally from the ancient regulations, made before the existence of Grand Lodges, and that what it does not possess, are the powers which were conceded by its predecessors to the Grand Lodge. This is evident from the history of warrants of constitution, the authority under which subordinate lodges act. The practice of applying by petition to the Grand Master or the Grand Lodge, for a warrant to meet as a regular lodge, commenced in the year 1718. Previous to that time, Freemasons were empowered by inherent privileges, vested, from time immemorial, in the whole fraternity, to meet as occasion might require, under the direction of some able architect; and the proceedings of these meetings, being approved by a majority of the Brethren convened at another lodge in the same district, were deemed constitutional[34]. But in 1718, a year after the formation of the Grand Lodge of England, this power of meeting *ad libitum* was resigned into the hands of that body, and it was then agreed that no lodges should thereafter meet, unless authorized so to do by a warrant from the Grand Master, and with the consent of the Grand Lodge. But as a memorial that this abandonment of the ancient right was entirely voluntary, it was at the same time resolved that this inherent privilege should continue to be enjoyed by the four old lodges who formed the Grand Lodge. And, still more effectually to secure the reserved rights of the lodges, it was also solemnly determined, that while the Grand Lodge possesses the inherent right of making new regulations for the good of the fraternity, provided that the *old landmarks be carefully preserved*, yet that these regulations, to be of force, must be proposed and agreed to at the third quarterly communication preceding the annual grand feast, and submitted to the perusal of all the Brethren, in writing, even of the youngest entered apprentice; "the approbation and consent of the majority of all the Brethren present being absolutely necessary, to make the same binding and obligatory.[35]"

The corollary from all this is clear. All the rights, powers, and privileges, not conceded, by express enactment of the fraternity,

---

34   Preston, Append., n. 4 (U.M.L., vol. iii., pp. 150, 151).
35   Book of Constitutions, orig. ed, p., 70 (U.M.L., vol. xv., book 1, p. 70).

to the Grand Lodge, have been reserved to themselves. Subordinate lodges are the assemblies of the craft in their primary capacity, and the Grand Lodge is the Supreme Masonic Tribunal, only because it consists of and is constituted by a representation of these primary assemblies. And, therefore, as every act of the Grand Lodge is an act of the whole fraternity thus represented, each new regulation that may be made is not an assumption of authority on the part of the Grand Lodge, but a new concession on the part of the subordinate lodges.

This doctrine of the reserved rights of the lodges is very important, and should never be forgotten, because it affords much aid in the decision of many obscure points of masonic jurisprudence. The rule is, that any doubtful power exists and is inherent in the subordinate lodges, unless there is an express regulation conferring it on the Grand Lodge. With this preliminary view, we may proceed to investigate the nature and extent of these reserved powers of the subordinate lodges.

A lodge has the right of selecting its own members, with which the Grand Lodge cannot interfere. This is a right that the lodges have expressly reserved to themselves, and the stipulation is inserted in the "general regulations" in the following words:

"No man can be entered a Brother in any particular lodge, or admitted a member thereof, without the unanimous consent of all the members of that lodge then present, when the candidate is proposed, and when their consent is formally asked by the Master. They are to give their consent in their own prudent way, either virtually or in form, but with unanimity. Nor is this inherent privilege subject to a dispensation, because the members of a particular lodge are the best judges of it; and because, if a turbu-

lent member should be imposed upon them, it might spoil their
harmony, or hinder the freedom of their communication; or even
break and disperse the lodge, which ought to be avoided by all
true and faithful.[36]"

But although a lodge has the inherent right to require unanimity in the election of a candidate, it is not necessarily restricted to such a degree of rigor.

A lodge has the right to elect its own officers. This right is
guaranteed to it by the words of the Warrant of Constitution. Still
the right is subject to certain restraining regulations. The election
must be held at the proper time, which, according to the usage of
Masonry, in most parts of the world, is on or immediately before
the festival of St. John the Evangelist. The proper qualifications
must be regarded. A member cannot be elected as Master, unless he has previously served as a Warden, except in the instance
of a new lodge, or other case of emergency. Where both of the
Wardens refuse promotion, where the presiding Master will not
permit himself to be reelected, and where there is no Past Master
who will consent to take the office, then, and then only, can a
member be elected from the floor to preside over the lodge.

By the Constitutions of England, only the Master and Treasurer are elected officers[37]. The Wardens and all the other officers

36   General Regulations of 1722. A subsequent regulation permitted theelection of a candidate, if there were not more than three black balls against him, provided the lodge desired
such a relaxation of the rule. The lodges of this country, however, very generally, and, as I
think, with
propriety, require unanimity. The subject will be hereafter discussed.
37   Every lodge shall annually elect its Master and Treasurer by ballot. Such Master having been regularly appointed and having served as Warden of a warranted lodge for one
year. _Constitutions of the Ancient Fraternity of Free and Accepted Masons, published by
authority of the United Grand Lodge of England_, 1847, _p_. 58 (U.M.L., vol. ix., book 1).

are appointed by the Master, who has not, however, the power of removal after appointment, except by consent of the lodge[38]; but American usage gives the election of all the officers, except the deacons, stewards, and, in some instances, the tiler, to the lodge.

As a consequence of the right of election, every lodge has the power of installing its officers, subject to the same regulations, in relation to time and qualifications, as given in the case of elections.

The Master must be installed by a Past Master[39], but after his own installation he has the power to install the rest of the officers. The ceremony of installation is not a mere vain and idle one, but is productive of important results. Until the Master and Wardens of a lodge are installed, they cannot represent the lodge in the Grand Lodge, nor, if it be a new lodge, can it be recorded and recognized on the register of the Grand Lodge. No officer can permanently take possession of the office to which he has been elected, until he has been duly installed[40]. The rule of the craft is, that the old officer holds on until his successor is installed, and this rule is of universal application to officers of every grade, from the Tiler of a subordinate lodge, to the Grand Master of Masons.

Every lodge that has been duly constituted, and its officers

---

38   The Wardens, or officers, of a lodge cannot be removed, unless for acause which appears to the lodge to be sufficient; but the Master, if he be dissatisfied with the conduct of any of his officers, may lay the cause of complaint before the lodge; and, if it shall appear to the majority of the Brethren present that the complaint be well founded, he shall have power to displa e such officer, and to nominate another. _English Constitutions, as above, p._ 80 (U.M.L., vol. ix., book 1).

39   It is not necessary that he should be a Past Master of the lodge.

40   No master shall assume the Master's chair, until he shall have been regularly installed, though he may in the interim rule the lodge. _English Constitutions_ (U.M.L., vol. ix., book 1).

installed, is entitled to be represented in the Grand Lodge, and to form, indeed, a constituent part of that body[41]. The representatives of a lodge are its Master and two Wardens[42]. This character of representation was established in 1718, when the four old lodges, which organized the Grand Lodge of England, agreed "to extend their patronage to every lodge which should hereafter be constituted by the Grand Lodge, according to the new regulations of the society; and while such lodges acted in conformity to the ancient constitutions of the Order, to admit their Masters and Wardens to share with them all the privileges of the Grand Lodge, excepting precedence of rank.[43]" Formerly all Master Masons were permitted to sit in the Grand Lodge, or, as it was then called, the General Assembly, and represent their lodge; and therefore this restricting the representation to the three superior officers was, in fact, a concession of the craft. This regulation is still generally observed; but I regret to see a few Grand Lodges in this country innovating on the usage, and still further confining the representation to the Masters alone.

The Master and Wardens are not merely in name the representatives of the lodge, but are bound, on all questions that come before the Grand Lodge, truly to represent their lodge, and vote according to its instructions. This doctrine is expressly laid down

41   Every Warranted Lodge is a constituent part of the Grand Lodge, in which assembly all the power of the fraternity resides. _English Constitutions, p_. 70 (U.M.L., vol. ix., book 1).

42   We shall not here discuss the question whether Past Masters aremembers of the Grand Lodge, by inherent right, as that subject will be more appropriately investigated when we come to speak of the Law of Grand Lodges, in a future chapter. They are, however clearly, not the
representatives of their lodge.

43   Preston, p. 167 (U.M.L., vol. iii., p. 151).

in the General Regulations, in the following words: "The majority of every particular lodge, when congregated, not else, shall have the privilege of giving instructions to their Master and Wardens, before the meeting of the Grand Chapter, or Quarterly Communication; because the said officers are their representatives, and are supposed to speak the sentiments of their Brethren at the said Grand Lodge.[44]"

Every lodge has the power to frame bye-laws for its own government, provided they are not contrary to, nor inconsistent with, the general regulations of the Grand Lodge; nor the landmarks of the order[45]. But these bye-laws will not be valid, until they are submitted to and approved by the Grand Lodge. And this is the case, also, with every subsequent alteration of them, which must in like manner be submitted to the Grand Lodge for its approval.

A lodge has the right of suspending or excluding a member from his membership in the lodge; but it has no power to expel him from the rights and privileges of Masonry, except with the consent of the Grand Lodge. A subordinate lodge tries its delinquent member, and, if guilty, declares him expelled; but the sentence is of no force until the Grand Lodge, under whose jurisdiction it is working, has confirmed it. And it is optional with the Grand Lodge to do so, or, as is frequently done, to reverse the decision and reinstate the Brother. Some of the lodges in this country claim the right to expel, independently of the action of the Grand Lodge; but the claim is not valid. The very fact that an expulsion is a penalty, affecting the general relations of the punished party with the whole fraternity, proves that its exercise

44   General Regulations. Of the duty of members, Art. X, (U.M.L., vol. xv., book 1, p. 61).
45   English Constitutions, p. 59 (U.M.L., vol. ix., book 1).

never could, with propriety, be intrusted to a body so circumscribed in its authority as a subordinate lodge. Accordingly, the general practice of the fraternity is opposed to it; and therefore all expulsions are reported to the Grand Lodge, not merely as matters of information, but that they may be confirmed by that body. The English Constitutions are explicit on this subject. "In the Grand Lodge alone," they declare, "resides the power of erasing lodges and expelling Brethren from the craft, a power which it ought not to delegate to any subordinate authority in England." They allow, however, a subordinate lodge to *exclude* a member from the lodge; in which case he is furnished with a certificate of the circumstances of his exclusion, and then may join any other lodge that will accept him, after being made acquainted with the fact of his exclusion, and its cause. This usage has not been adopted in this country.

A lodge has a right to levy such annual contribution for membership as the majority of the Brethren see fit. This is entirely a matter of contract, with which the Grand Lodge, or the craft in general, have nothing to do. It is, indeed, a modern usage, unknown to the fraternity of former times, and was instituted for the convenience and support of the private lodges.

A lodge is entitled to select a name for itself, to be, however, approved by the Grand Lodge[46]. But the Grand Lodge alone has the power of designating the number by which the lodge shall be distinguished. By its number alone is every lodge recognized in the register of the Grand Lodge, and according to their numbers is the precedence of the lodges regulated.

---

46   In selecting the name, the modern Constitutions of England make the approbation of the Grand Master or Provincial Grand Master necessary.

Finally, a lodge has certain rights in relation to its Warrant of Constitution. This instrument having been granted by the Grand Lodge, can be revoked by no other authority. The Grand Master, therefore, has no power, as he has in the case of a lodge under dispensation, to withdraw its Warrant, except temporarily, until the next meeting of the Grand Lodge. Nor is it in the power of even the majority of the lodge, by any act of their own, to resign the Warrant. For it has been laid down as a law, that if the majority of the lodge should determine to quit the lodge, or to resign their warrant, such action would be of no efficacy, because the Warrant of Constitution, and the power of assembling, would remain with the rest of the members, who adhere to their allegiance[47]. But if all the members withdraw themselves, their Warrant ceases and becomes extinct. If the conduct of a lodge has been such as clearly to forfeit its charter, the Grand Lodge alone can decide that question and pronounce the forfeiture.

Section II.
Of the Duties of a Lodge.

So far in relation to the rights and privileges of subordinate lodges. But there are certain duties and obligations equally binding upon these bodies, and certain powers, in the exercise of which they are restricted. These will next engage our attention.

The first great duty, not only of every lodge, but of every Mason, is to see that the landmarks of the Order shall never be impaired. The General Regulations of Masonry--to which every Master, at his installation, is bound to acknowledge his submis-

47   Such is the doctrine of the modern English Constitutions.

sion--declare that "it is not in the power of any man, or body of men, to make innovations in the body of Masonry." And, hence, no lodge, without violating all the implied and express obligations into which it has entered, can, in any manner, alter or amend the work, lectures, and ceremonies of the institution. As its members have received the ritual from their predecessors, so are they bound to transmit it, unchanged, in the slightest degree, to their successors. In the Grand Lodge, alone, resides the power of enacting new regulations; but, even *it* must be careful that, in every such regulation, the landmarks are preserved. When, therefore, we hear young and inexperienced Masters speak of making improvements (as they arrogantly call them) upon the old lectures or ceremonies, we may be sure that such Masters either know nothing of the duties they owe to the craft, or are willfully forgetful of the solemn obligation which they have contracted. Some may suppose that the ancient ritual of the Order is imperfect, and requires amendment. One may think that the ceremonies are too simple, and wish to increase them; another, that they are too complicated, and desire to simplify them; one may be displeased with the antiquated language; another, with the character of the traditions; a third, with something else. But, the rule is imperative and absolute, that no change can or must be made to gratify individual taste. As the Barons of England, once, with unanimous voice, exclaimed, "Nolumus leges Angliae mutare!" so do all good Masons respond to every attempt at innovation, "We are unwilling to alter the customs of Freemasonry."

In relation to the election of officers, a subordinate lodge is allowed to exercise no discretion. The names and duties of these officers are prescribed, partly by the landmarks or the ancient constitutions, and partly by the regulations of various Grand Lodges. While the landmarks are preserved, a Grand Lodge may add to the list of officers as it pleases; and whatever may be its regulation, the subordinate lodges are bound to obey it; nor can any such lodge create new offices nor abolish old ones without the consent of the Grand Lodge.

Lodges are also bound to elect their officers at a time which is always determined; not by the subordinate, but by the Grand Lodge. Nor can a lodge anticipate or postpone it unless by a dispensation from the Grand Master.

No lodge can, at an extra meeting, alter or amend the proceedings of a regular meeting. If such were not the rule, an unworthy Master might, by stealth, convoke an extra meeting of a part of his lodge, and, by expunging or altering the proceedings of the previous regular meeting, or any particular part of them, annul any measures or resolutions that were not consonant with his peculiar views.

No lodge can interfere with the work or business of any other lodge, without its permission. This is an old regulation, founded on those principles of comity and brotherly love that should exist among all Masons. It is declared in the manuscript charges, written in the reign of James II., and in the possession of the Lodge of Antiquity, at London, that "no Master or Fellow shall supplant others of their work; that is to say, that, if he hath taken a work, or else stand Master of any work, that he shall not put him out, unless he be unable of cunning to make an end of his work." And, hence, no lodge can pass or raise a candidate who was initiated, or initiate one who was rejected, in another lodge. "It would be highly improper," says the Ahiman Rezon, "in any lodge, to confer a degree on a Brother who is not of their house-hold; for, every lodge ought to be competent to manage their own business, and are the best judges of the qualifications of their own members."

I do not intend, at the present time, to investigate the qualifications of candidates--as that subject will, in itself, afford ample materials for a future investigation; but, it is necessary that I should say something of the restrictions under which every lodge labors in respect to the admission of persons applying for degrees.

In the first place, no lodge can initiate a candidate, "without previous notice, and due examination into his character; and not unless his petition has been read at one regular meeting and acted on at another." This is in accordance with the ancient regulations; but, an exception to it is allowed in the case of an emergency, when the lodge may read the petition for admission, and, if the applicant is well recommended, may proceed at once to elect and initiate him. In some jurisdictions, the nature of the emergency must be stated to the Grand Master, who, if he approves, will grant a dispensation; but, in others, the Master, or Master and Wardens, are permitted to be competent judges, and may proceed to elect and initiate, without such dispensation. The Grand Lodge of South Carolina adheres to the former custom, and that of England to the latter.

Another regulation is, that no lodge can confer more than two degrees, at one communication, on the same candidate. The Grand Lodge of England is still more stringent on this subject, and declares that "no candidate shall be permitted to receive more than one degree, on the same day; nor shall a higher degree in Masonry be conferred on any Brother at a less interval than four weeks from his receiving a previous degree, nor until he has passed an examination, in open lodge, in that degree." This rule is also in force in South Carolina and several other of the American jurisdictions. But, the law which forbids the whole three degrees of Ancient Craft Masonry to be conferred, at the same communication, on one candidate, is universal in its application, and, as such, may be deemed one of the ancient landmarks of the Order.

There is another rule, which seems to be of universal extent, and is, indeed, contained in the General Regulations of 1767, to the following effect: "No lodge shall make more than five new Brothers at one and the same time, without an urgent necessity."

All lodges are bound to hold their meetings at least once in every calendar month; and every lodge neglecting so to do for one year, thereby forfeits its warrant of constitution.

The subject of the removal of lodges is the last thing that shall engage our attention. Here the ancient regulations of the craft have adopted many guards to prevent the capricious or improper removal of a lodge from its regular place of meeting. In the first place, no lodge can be removed from the town in which it is situated, to any other place, without the consent of the Grand Lodge. But, a lodge may remove from one part of the town to another, with the consent of the members, under the following restrictions: The removal cannot be made without the Master's knowledge; nor can any motion, for that purpose, be presented in his absence. When such a motion is made, and properly seconded, the Master will order summonses to every member, specifying the business, and appointing a day for considering and determining the affair. And if then a majority of the lodge, with the Master, or two-thirds, without him, consent to the removal, it shall take place; but notice thereof must be sent, at once, to the Grand Lodge. The General Regulations of 1767 further declare, that such removal must be approved by the Grand Master. I suppose that where the removal of the lodge was only a matter of convenience to the members, the Grand Lodge would hardly interfere, but leave the whole subject to their discretion; but, where the removal would be calculated to affect the interests of the lodge, or of the fraternity--as in the case of a removal to a house of bad reputation, or to a place of evident insecurity--I have no doubt that the Grand Lodge, as the conservator of the character and safety of the institution, would have a right to interpose its authority, and prevent the improper removal.

I have thus treated, as concisely as the important nature of the subjects would permit, of the powers, privileges, duties, and obligations of lodges, and have endeavored to embrace, within the limits of the discussion, all those prominent principles of the Order, which, as they affect the character and operations of the craft in their primary assemblies, may properly be referred to the Law of Subordinate Lodges.

Chapter IV.
Of the Officers of a Subordinate Lodge.

Section I.
Of the Officers in General.

Four officers, at least, the ancient customs of the craft require in every lodge; and they are consequently found throughout the globe. These are the Master, the two Wardens, and the Tiler. Almost equally universal are the offices of Treasurer, Secretary, and two Deacons. But, besides these, there may be additional officers appointed by different Grand Lodges. The Grand Lodge of England, for instance, requires the appointment of an officer, called the "Inner Guard." The Grand Orient of France has prescribed a variety of officers, which are unknown to English and American Masonry. The Grand Lodges of England and South Carolina direct that two Stewards shall be appointed, while some other Grand Lodges make no such requisition. Ancient usage seems to have recognized the following officers of a subordinate lodge: the Master, two Wardens, Treasurer, Secretary, two Deacons, two Stewards, and Tiler; and I shall therefore treat of the duties and powers of these officers only, in the course of the present chapter.

The officers of a lodge are elected annually. In this country, the election takes place on the festival of St. John the Evangelist, or at the meeting immediately previous; but, in this latter case, the duties of the offices do not commence until St. John's day, which may, therefore, be considered as the beginning of the masonic year.

Dalcho lays down the rule, that "no Freemason chosen into any office can refuse to serve (unless he has before filled the same office), without incurring the penalties established by the bye-laws." Undoubtedly a lodge may enact such a regulation, and affix any reasonable penalty; but I am not aware of any ancient regulation which makes it incumbent on subordinate lodges to do so.

If any of the subordinate officers, except the Master and Wardens, die, or be removed from office, during the year, the lodge may, under the authority of a dispensation from the Grand Master, enter into an election to supply the vacancy. But in the case of the death or removal of the Master or either of the Wardens, no election can be held to supply the vacancy, even by dispensation, for reasons which will appear when I come to treat of those offices.

No officer can resign his office after he has been installed. Every officer is elected for twelve months, and at his installation solemnly promises to perform the duties of that office until the next regular day of election; and hence the lodge cannot permit him, by a resignation, to violate his obligation of office.

Another rule is, that every officer holds on to his office until his successor has been installed. It is the installation, and not the election, which puts an officer into possession; and the faithful management of the affairs of Masonry requires, that between the election and installation of his successor, the predecessor shall not vacate the office, but continue to discharge its duties.

An office can be vacated only by death, permanent removal from the jurisdiction, or expulsion. Suspension does not vacate, but only suspends the performance of the duties of the office, which must then be temporarily discharged by some other person, to be appointed from time to time; for, as soon as the suspended officer is restored, he resumes the dignities and duties of his office.

Section II.
Of the Worshipful Master.

This is probably the most important office in the whole system of Masonry, as, upon the intelligence, skill, and fidelity of the Masters of our lodges, the entire institution is dependent for its prosperity. It is an office which is charged with heavy responsibilities, and, as a just consequence, is accompanied by the investiture of many important powers.

A necessary qualification of the Master of a lodge is, that he must have previously served in the office of a Warden[48]. This qualification is sometimes dispensed with in the case of new lodges, or where no member of an old lodge, who has served as a Warden, will accept the office of Master. But it is not necessary that he should have served as a Warden in the lodge of which he is proposed to be elected Master. The discharge of the duties of a Warden, by regular election and installation in any other lodge, and at any former period, will be a sufficient qualification.

One of the most important duties of the Master of a lodge is, to see that the edicts and regulations of the Grand Lodge are obeyed by his Brethren, and that his officers faithfully discharge their duties.

The Master has particularly in charge the warrant of Constitution, which must always be present in his lodge, when opened.

The Master has a right to call a special meeting of his lodge whenever he pleases, and is the sole judge of any emergency which may require such special communication.

He has, also, the right of closing his lodge at any hour that he may deem expedient, notwithstanding the whole business of the evening may not have been transacted. This regulation arises

---

48   "No Brother can be a Warden until he has passed the part of a Fellow Craft; nor a Master until he has acted as a Warden."--_Old Charges_, IV. (U.M.L., vol. xv., book 1, p. 52).

from the unwritten law of Masonry. As the Master is responsible to the Grand Lodge for the fidelity of the work done in his lodge, and as the whole of the labor is, therefore, performed under his superintendence, it follows that, to enable him to discharge this responsibility, he must be invested with the power of commencing, of continuing, or of suspending labor at such time as he may, in his wisdom, deem to be the most advantageous to the edifice of Masonry.

It follows from this rule that a question of adjournment cannot be entertained in a lodge. The adoption of a resolution to adjourn, would involve the necessity of the Master to obey it. The power, therefore, of controlling the work, would be taken out of his hands and placed in those of the members, which would be in direct conflict with the duties imposed upon him by the ritual. The doctrine that a lodge cannot adjourn, but must be closed or called off at the pleasure of the Master, appears now to me to be very generally admitted.

The Master and his two Wardens constitute the representatives of the lodge in the Grand Lodge, and it is his duty to attend the communications of that body "on all convenient occasions.[49]" When there, he is faithfully to represent his lodge, and on all questions discussed, to obey its instructions, voting in every case rather against his own convictions than against the expressed wish of his lodge.

The Master presides not only over the symbolic work of the lodge, but also over its business deliberations, and in either case his decisions are reversible only by the Grand Lodge. There can be no appeal from his decision, on any question, to the lodge. He

---

49   Regulations on Installation of a Master, No. III. Preston, p. 74 (U.M.L., vol. iii., p. 61).

is supreme in his lodge, so far as the lodge is concerned, being amenable for his conduct in the government of it, not to its members, but to the Grrand Lodge alone. If an appeal were proposed, it would be his duty, for the preservation of discipline, to refuse to put the question. If a member is aggrieved by the conduct or decisions of the Master, he has his redress by an appeal to the Grrand Lodge, which will, of course, see that the Master does not rule his lodge "in an unjust or arbitrary manner." But such a thing as an appeal from the Master of the lodge to its members is unknown in Masonry.

This may, at first sight, appear to be giving too despotic power to the Master. But a slight reflection will convince any one that there can be but little danger of oppression from one so guarded and controlled as a Master is, by the sacred obligations of his office, and the supervision of the Grand Lodge, while the placing in the hands of the craft so powerful, and at times, and with bad spirits, so annoying a privilege as that of immediate appeal, would necessarily tend to impair the energies and lessen the dignity of the Master, while it would be subversive of that spirit of discipline which pervades every part of the institution, and to which it is mainly indebted for its prosperity and perpetuity.

The ancient charges rehearsed at the installation of a Master, prescribe the various moral qualifications which are required in the aspirant for that elevated and responsible office. He is to be a good man, and peaceable citizen or subject, a respecter of the laws, and a lover of his Brethren--cultivating the social virtues and promoting the general good of society as well as of his own Order.

Within the last few years, the standard of intellectual qualifications has been greatly elevated. And it is now admitted that the Master of a lodge, to do justice to the exalted office which he holds, to the craft over whom he presides, and to the candidates whom he is to instruct, should be not only a man of irreproachable moral character, but also of expanded intellect and liberal education. Still, as there is no express law upon this subject, the selection of a Master and the determination of his qualifications must be left to the judgment and good sense of the members.

Section III.
Of the Wardens.

The Senior and Junior Warden are the assistants of the Master in the government of the lodge. They are selected from among the members on the floor, the possession of a previous office not being, as in the case of the Master, a necessary qualification for election. In England they are appointed by the Master, but in this country they are universally elected by the lodge.

During the temporary absence of the Master the Senior Warden has the right of presiding, though he may, and often does by courtesy, invite a Past Master to assume the chair. In like manner, in the absence of both Master and Senior Warden, the Junior Warden will preside, and competent Brethren will by him be appointed to fill the vacant seats of the Wardens. But if the Master and Junior Warden be present, and the Senior Warden be absent, the Junior Warden does not occupy the West, but retains his own station, the Master appointing some Brother to occupy the station of the Senior Warden. For the Junior Warden succeeds by law only to the office of Master, and, unless that office be vacant, he is bound to fulfill the duties of the office to which he has been obligated.

In case of the death, removal from the jurisdiction, or expulsion of the Master, by the Grand Lodge, no election can be held until the constitutional period. The Senior Warden will take the Master's place and preside over the lodge, while his seat will be temporarily filled from time to time by appointment. The Senior Warden being in fact still in existence, and only discharging one of the highest duties of his office, that of presiding in the absence of the Master, his office cannot be declared vacant and there can be no election for it. In such case, the Junior Warden, for the reason already assigned, will continue at his own station in the South.

In case of the death, removal, or expulsion of both Master and Senior Warden, the Junior Warden will discharge the duties of the Mastership and make temporary appointments of both Wardens. It must always be remembered that the Wardens succeed according to seniority to the office of Master when vacant, but that neither can legally discharge the duties of the other. It must also be remembered that when a Warden succeeds to the government of the lodge, he does not become the Master; he is still only a Warden discharging the functions of a higher vacated station, as one of the expressed duties of his own office. A recollection of these distinctions will enable us to avoid much embarrassment in the consideration of all the questions incident to this subject. If the Master be present, the Wardens assist him in the government of the lodge. The Senior Warden presides over the craft while at labor, and the Junior when they are in refreshment. Formerly the examination of visitors was intrusted to the Junior Warden, but this duty is now more appropriately performed by the Stewards or a special committee appointed for that purpose.

The Senior Warden has the appointment of the Senior Deacon, and the Junior Warden that of the Stewards.

Section IV.
Of the Treasurer.

Of so much importance is this office deemed, that in English Lodges, while all the other officers are appointed by the Master, the Treasurer alone is elected by the lodge. It is, however, singular, that in the ritual of installation, Preston furnishes no address to the Treasurer on his investiture. Webb, however, has supplied the omission, and the charge given in his work to this officer, on the night of his installation, having been universally acknowledged and adopted by the craft in this country, will furnish us with the most important points of the law in relation to his duties.

It is, then, in the first place, the duty of the Treasurer "to receive all moneys from the hands of the Secretary." The Treasurer is only the banker of the lodge. All fees for initiation, arrearages of members, and all other dues to the lodge, should be first received by the Secretary, and paid immediately over to the Treasurer for safe keeping.

The keeping of just and regular accounts is another duty presented to the Treasurer. As soon as he has received an amount of money from the Secretary, he should transfer the account of it to his books. By this means, the Secretary and Treasurer become mutual checks upon each other, and the safety of the funds of the lodge is secured.

The Treasurer is not only the banker, but also the disbursing officer of the lodge; but he is directed to pay no money except with the consent of the lodge and on the order of the Worshipful Master. It seems to me, therefore, that every warrant drawn on him should be signed by the Master, and the action of the lodge attested by the counter-signature of the Secretary.

It is usual, in consequence of the great responsibility of the Treasurer, to select some Brother of worldly substance for the office; and still further to insure the safety of the funds, by exacting from him a bond, with sufficient security. He sometimes receives a per centage, or a fixed salary, for his services.

Section V.
Of the Secretary.

It is the duty of the Secretary to record all the proceedings of the lodge, "which may be committed to paper;" to conduct the correspondence of the lodge, and to receive all moneys due the lodge from any source whatsoever. He is, therefore, the recording, corresponding, and receiving officer of the lodge. By receiving the moneys due to the lodge in the first place, and then paying them over to the Treasurer, he becomes, as I have already observed, a check upon that officer.

In view of the many laborious duties which devolve upon him, the Secretary, in many lodges, receives a compensation for his services.

Should the Treasurer or Secretary die or be expelled, there is no doubt that an election for a successor, to fill the unexpired

term, may be held by dispensation from the Grand Master. But
the incompetency of either of these officers to perform his duties,
by reason of the infirmity of sickness or removal from the seat of
the lodge, will not, I think, authorize such an election. Because
the original officer may recover from his infirmity, or return to his
residence, and, in either case, having been elected and installed
for one year, he must remain the Secretary or Treasurer until the
expiration of the period for which he had been so elected and
installed, and, therefore, on his recovery or his return, is entitled
to resume all the prerogatives and functions of his office. The
case of death, or of expulsion, which is, in fact, masonic death,
is different, because all the rights possessed during life cease *ex
necessitate rei*, and forever lapse at the time of the said physical or
masonic death; and in the latter case, a restoration to all the rights
and privileges of Masonry would not restore the party to any office which he had held at the time of his expulsion.

Section VI.
Of the Deacons.

In every lodge there are two of these officers--a Senior and a
Junior Deacon. They are not elected, but appointed; the former
by the Master, and the latter by the Senior Warden.

The duties of these officers are many and important; but they
are so well defined in the ritual as to require no further consideration in this place.

The only question that here invites our examination is, whether the Deacons, as appointed officers, are removable at the pleasure of the officers who appointed them; or, whether they retain

their offices, like the Master and Wardens, until the expiration of the year. Masonic authorities are silent on this subject; but, basing my judgment upon analogy, I am inclined to think that they are not removable: all the officers of a lodge are chosen to serve for one year, or, from one festival of St. John the Evangelist to the succeeding one. This has been the invariable usage in all lodges, and neither in the monitorial ceremonies of installation, nor in any rules or regulations which I have seen, is any exception to this usage made in respect to Deacons. The written as well as the oral law of Masonry being silent on this subject, we are bound to give them the benefit of this silence, and place them in the same favorable position as that occupied by the superior officers, who, we know, by express law are entitled to occupy their stations for one year. Moreover, the power of removal is too important to be exercised except under the sanction of an expressed law, and is contrary to the whole spirit of Masonry, which, while it invests a presiding officer with the largest extent of prerogative, is equally careful of the rights of the youngest member of the fraternity.

From these reasons I am compelled to believe that the Deacons, although originally appointed by the Master and Senior Warden, are not removable by either, but retain their offices until the expiration of the year.

Section VII.
Of the Stewards.

The Stewards, who are two in number, are appointed by the Junior Warden, and sit on the right and left of him in the lodge. Their original duties were, "to assist in the collection of dues and subscriptions; to keep an account of the lodge expenses; to see that the tables are properly furnished at refreshment, and that every Brother is suitably provided for." They are also considered as the assistants of the Deacons in the discharge of their duties, and, lately, some lodges are beginning to confide to them the important trusts of a standing committee for the examination of visitors and the preparation of candidates.

What has been said in relation to the removal of the Deacons in the preceding section, is equally applicable to the Stewards.

Section VIII.
Of the Tiler.

This is an office of great importance, and must, from the peculiar nature of our institution, have existed from its very beginning. No lodge could ever have been opened until a Tiler was appointed, and stationed to guard its portals from the approach of "cowans and eavesdroppers." The qualifications requisite for the office of a Tiler are, that he must be "a worthy Master Mason." An Entered Apprentice, or a Fellow Craft, cannot tile a lodge, even though it be opened in his own degree. To none but Master Masons can this important duty of guardianship be intrusted. The Tiler is not necessarily a member of the lodge which he tiles. There is no regulation requiring this qualification. In fact, in large cities, one Brother often acts as the Tiler of several lodges. If, however, he is a member of the lodge, his office does not deprive him of the rights of membership, and in ballotings for candidates, election of officers, or other important questions, he is entitled to exercise his privilege of voting, in which case the Junior Deacon will temporarily occupy his station, while he enters the lodge to deposit his ballot. This appears to be the general usage of the craft in this country.

The Tiler is sometimes elected by the lodge, and sometimes appointed by the Master. It seems generally to be admitted that he may be removed from office for misconduct or neglect of duty, by the lodge, if he has been elected, and by the Master, if he has been appointed.

Chapter V.
Of Rules of Order.

The safety of the minority, the preservation of harmony, and the dispatch of business, all require that there should be, in every well-regulated society, some rules and forms for the government of their proceedings, and, as has been justly observed by an able writer on parliamentary law, "whether these forms be in all cases the most rational or not, is really not of so great importance; for it is much more material that there should be a rule to go by, than what that rule is.[50]" By common consent, the rules established for the government of Parliament in England, and of Congress in the United States, and which are known collectively under the name of "Parliamentary Law," have been adopted for the regulation of all deliberative bodies, whether of a public or private nature. But lodges of Freemasons differ so much in their organization and character from other societies, that this law will, in very few cases, be found applicable; and, indeed, in many positively inap-

---

50   Hats. quoted in Jefferson, p. 14.

plicable to them. The rules, therefore, for the government of masonic lodges are in general to be deduced from the usages of the
Order, from traditional or written authority, and where both of
them are silent, from analogy to the character of the institution.
To each of these sources, therefore, I shall apply, in the course of
the present chapter, and in some few instances, where the parliamentary law coincides with our own, reference will be made to
the authority of the best writers on that science.

Section I.
Of the Order of Business.

When the Brethren have been "congregated," or called together by the presiding officer, the first thing to be attended to
is the ceremony of opening the lodge. The consideration of this
subject, as it is sufficiently detailed in our ritual, will form no part
of the present work.

The lodge having been opened, the next thing to be attended to is the reading of the minutes of the last communication.
The minutes having been read, the presiding officer will put the
question on their confirmation, having first inquired of the Senior and Junior Wardens, and lastly of the Brethren "around the
lodge," whether they have any alterations to propose. It must be
borne in mind, that the question of confirmation is simply a question whether the Secretary has faithfully and correctly recorded
the transactions of the lodge. If, therefore, it can be satisfactorily
shown by any one that there is a mis-entry, or the omission of
an entry, this is the time to correct it; and where the matter is
of sufficient importance, and the recording officer, or any mem-

ber disputes the charge of error, the vote of the lodge will be taken on the subject, and the journal will be amended or remain as written, according to the opinion so expressed by the majority of the members. As this is, however, a mere question of memory, it must be apparent that those members only who were present at the previous communication, the records of which are under examination, are qualified to express a fair opinion. All others should ask and be permitted to be excused from voting.

As no special communication can alter or amend the proceedings of a regular one, it is not deemed necessary to present the records of the latter to the inspection of the former. This preliminary reading of the minutes is, therefore, always omitted at special communications.

After the reading of the minutes, unfinished business, such as motions previously submitted and reports of committees previously appointed, will take the preference of all other matters. Special communications being called for the consideration of some special subject, that subject must of course claim the priority of consideration over all others.

In like manner, where any business has been specially and specifically postponed to another communication, it constitutes at that communication what is called, in parliamentary law, "the order of the day," and may at any time in the course of the evening be called up, to the exclusion of all other business.

The lodge may, however, at its discretion, refuse to take up the consideration of such order; for the same body which determined at one time to consider a question, may at another time refuse to do so. This is one of those instances in which parliamentary usage is applicable to the government of a lodge. Jefferson says: "Where an order is made, that any particular matter be taken up on any particular day, there a question is to be put, when it is called for, Whether the house will now proceed to that matter?" In a lodge, however, it is not the usage to propose such a question, but the matter being called up, is discussed and acted on, unless some Brother moves its postponement, when the question of postponement is put.

But with these exceptions, the unfinished business must first be disposed of, to avoid its accumulation and its possible subsequent neglect[51].

New business will then be taken up in such order as the local bye-laws prescribe, or the wisdom of the Worshipful Master may suggest.

In a discussion, when any member wishes to speak, he must stand up in his place, and address himself not to the lodge, nor to any particular Brother, but to the presiding officer, styling him "Worshipful."

When two or more members rise nearly together, the presiding officer determines who is entitled to speak, and calls him by his name, whereupon he proceeds, unless he voluntarily sits down, and gives way to the other. The ordinary rules of courtesy, which should govern a masonic body above all other societies, as well as the general usage of deliberative bodies, require that the one first up should be entitled to the floor. But the decision of this fact is left entirely to the Master, or presiding officer.

Whether a member be entitled to speak once or twice to the

---

51   One of the ancient charges, which Preston tells us that it was the constant practice of our Ancient Brethren to rehearse at the opening and closing of the lodge, seems to refer to this rule, when it says, "the Master, Wardens, and Brethren are just and faithful, and _carefully finish the work they begin_."--Oliver's Preston, p. 27, _note_ (U.M.L., vol. iii., p. 22).

same question, is left to the regulation of the local bye-laws of every lodge. But, under all circumstances, it seems to be conceded, that a member may rise at any time with the permission of the presiding officer, or for the purpose of explanation.

A member may be called to order by any other while speaking, for the use of any indecorous remark, personal allusion, or irrelevant matter; but this must be done in a courteous and conciliatory manner, and the question of order will at once be decided by the presiding officer.

No Brother is to be interrupted while speaking, except for the purpose of calling him to order, or to make a necessary explanation; nor are any separate conversations, or, as they are called in our ancient charges, "private committees," to be allowed.

Every member of the Order is, in the course of the debate as well as at all other times in the lodge, to be addressed by the title of "Brother," and no secular or worldly titles are ever to be used.

In accordance with the principles of justice, the parliamentary usage is adopted, which permits the mover of a resolution to make the concluding speech, that he may reply to all those who have spoken against it, and sum up the arguments in its favor. And it would be a breach of order as well as of courtesy for any of his opponents to respond to this final argument of the mover.

It is within the discretion of the Master, at any time in the course of the evening, to suspend the business of the lodge for the purpose of proceeding to the ceremony of initiation, for the "work" of Masonry, as it is technically called, takes precedence of all other business.

When all business, both old and new, and the initiation of candidates, if there be any, has been disposed of, the presiding officer inquires of the officers and members if there be anything more to be proposed before closing. Custom has prescribed a formulary for making this inquiry, which is in the following words.

The Worshipful Master, addressing the Senior and Junior Wardens and then the Brethren, successively, says: "Brother Senior, have you anything to offer in the West for the good of Masonry in general or of this lodge in particular? Anything in the South, Brother Junior? Around the lodge, Brethren?" The answers to these inquiries being in the negative on the part of the Wardens, and silence on that of the craft, the Master proceeds to close the lodge in the manner prescribed in the ritual.

The reading of the minutes of the evening, not for confirmation, but for suggestion, lest anything may have been omitted, should always precede the closing ceremonies, unless, from the lateness of the hour, it be dispensed with by the members.

Section II.

Of Appeals from the Decision of the Chair.

Freemasonry differs from all other institutions, in permitting no appeal to the lodge from the decision of the presiding officer. The Master is supreme in his lodge, so far as the lodge is concerned. He is amenable for his conduct, in the government of the lodge, not to its members, but to the Grand Lodge alone. In deciding points of order as well as graver matters, no appeal can be taken from that decision to the lodge. If an appeal were proposed, it would be his duty, for the preservation of discipline, to refuse to put the question. It is, in fact, wrong that the Master should even by courtesy permit such an appeal to be taken; because, as the

Committee of Correspondence of the Grand Lodge of Tennessee have wisely remarked, by the admission of such appeals by *courtesy*, "is established ultimately a precedent from which will be claimed *the right to take* appeals.[52]" If a member is aggrieved with the conduct or the decisions of the Master, he has his redress by an appeal to the Grand Lodge, which will of course see that the Master does not rule his lodge "in an unjust or arbitrary manner." But such a thing as an appeal from the Master to the lodge is unknown in Masonry.

This, at first view, may appear to be giving too despotic a power to the Master. But a little reflection will convince any one that there can be but slight danger of oppression from one so guarded and controlled as the Master is by the obligations of his office and the superintendence of the Grand Lodge, while the placing in the hands of the craft so powerful, and, with bad spirits, so annoying a privilege as that of immediate appeal, would necessarily tend to impair the energies and lessen the dignity of the Master, at the same time that it would be totally subversive of that spirit of strict discipline which pervades every part of the institution, and to which it is mainly indebted for its prosperity and perpetuity.

In every case where a member supposes himself to be aggrieved by the decision of the Master, he should make his appeal to the Grand Lodge.

It is scarcely necessary to add, that a Warden or Past Master, presiding in the absence of the Master, assumes for the time all the rights and prerogatives of the Master.

---

52   Proceedings of G.L. of Tennessee, 1850. Appendix A, p. 8.

Section III.
Of the Mode of Taking the Question.

The question in Masonry is not taken *viva voce* or by "aye" and "nay." This should always be done by "a show of hands." The regulation on this subject was adopted not later than the year 1754, at which time the Book of Constitutions was revised, "and the necessary alterations and additions made, consistent with the laws and rules of Masonry," and accordingly, in the edition published in the following year, the regulation is laid down in these words--"The opinions or votes of the members are always to be signified by each holding up one of his hands: which uplifted hands the Grand Wardens are to count; unless the number of hands be so unequal as to render the counting useless. Nor should any other kind of division be ever admitted among Masons.[53]"

Calling for the yeas and nays has been almost universally condemned as an unmasonic practice, nor should any Master allow it to be resorted to in his lodge.

Moving the "previous question," a parliamentary invention for stopping all discussion, is still more at variance with the liberal and harmonious spirit which should distinguish masonic debates, and is, therefore, never to be permitted in a lodge.

Section IV.
Of Adjournments.

Adjournment is a term not recognized in Masonry. There are

---

53   Book of Constitutions, edition of 1755, p. 282.

but two ways in which the communication of a lodge can be terminated; and these are either by *closing* the lodge, or by *calling
from labor to refreshment*. In the former case the business of the
communication is finally disposed of until the next communication; in the latter the lodge is still supposed to be open and may
resume its labors at any time indicated by the Master.

But both the time of closing the lodge and of calling it from
labor to refreshment is to be determined by the absolute will and
the free judgment of the Worshipful Master, to whom alone is
intrusted the care of "setting the craft to work, and giving them
wholesome instruction for labor." He alone is responsible to the
Grand Master and the Grand Lodge, that his lodge shall be opened,
continued, and closed in harmony; and as it is by his "will and
pleasure" only that it is opened, so is it by his "will and pleasure"
only that it can be closed. Any attempt, therefore, on the part
of the lodge to entertain a motion for adjournment would be an
infringement of this prerogative of the Master. Such a motion
is, therefore, always out of order, and cannot be; and cannot be
acted on.

The rule that a lodge cannot adjourn, but remain in session
until closed by the Master, derives an authoritative sanction also
from the following clause in the fifth of the Old Charges.

"All Masons employed shall meekly receive their wages without murmuring or mutiny, *and not desert the Master till the work is
finished*."

Section V.
Of the Appointment of Committees.

It is the prerogative of the Master to appoint all Committees, unless by a special resolution provision has been made that a committee shall otherwise be appointed.

The Master is also, *ex officio*, chairman of every committee which he chooses to attend, although he may not originally have been named a member of such committee. But he may, if he chooses, waive this privilege; yet he may, at any time during the session of the committee, reassume his inherent prerogative of governing the craft at all times when in his presence, and therefore take the chair.

Section VI.
Of the Mode of Keeping the Minutes.

Masonry is preeminently an institution of forms, and hence, as was to be expected, there is a particular form provided for recording the proceedings of a lodge. Perhaps the best method of communicating this form to the reader will be, to record the proceedings of a supposititious meeting or communication.

The following form, therefore, embraces the most important transactions that usually occur during the session of a lodge, and it may serve as an exemplar, for the use of secretaries.

"A regular communication of ---- Lodge, NO. ----, was holden at ----; on ----, the ---- day of ----A.: L.: 58--.

Present.

Bro.: A. B----, W.: Master.
"   B. C----, S.: Warden.
"   C. D----, J.: Warden.
"   D. E----, Treasurer.
"   E. F----, Secretary.
"   F. G----, S.: Deacon.
"   G. H----, J.: Deacon.
"   H. I----, } Stewards.
"   I. K----, }
"   K. L----, Tiler.

Members.
Bro.: L. M----
      M. N----
      N. O----
      O. P----

Visitors.
      P. Q----
      Q. R----
      R. S----

      S. T----
The Lodge was opened in due form on the third degree of

Masonry.

"The minutes of the regular communication of ---- were read and confirmed[54].

"The committee on the petition of Mr. C. B., a candidate for initiation, reported favorably, whereupon he was balloted for and duly elected.

"The committee on the application of Mr. D. C., a candidate for initiation, reported favorably, whereupon he was balloted for, and the box appearing foul he was rejected.

"The committee on the application of Mr. E. D., a candidate for initiation, having reported unfavorably, he was declared rejected without a ballot.

"The petition of Mr. F. E., a candidate for initiation, having been withdrawn by his friends, he was declared rejected without a ballot.

"A petition for initiation from Mr. G.F., inclosing the usual amount and recommended by Bros. C. D.---- and H. I.----, was referred to a committee of investigation consisting of Bros. G. H.----, L. M.----, and O. P.----.

"Bro. S.R., an Entered Apprentice, having applied for advancement, was duly elected to take the second degree; and Bro. W.Y., a Fellow Craft, was, on his application for advancement, duly elected to take the third degree.

"A letter was read from Mrs. T. V.----, the widow of a Master Mason, when the sum of twenty dollars was voted for her relief.

"The amendment to article 10, section 5 of the bye-laws, proposed by Bro. M. N. ---- at the communication of ----, was read a

---

54   If it is an extra communication, this item of the transaction is, of course, omitted, for minutes are only to be confirmed at regular communications.

third time, adopted by a constitutional majority and ordered to be sent to the Grand Lodge for approval and confirmation.

"The Lodge of Master Masons was then closed, and a lodge of Entered Apprentices opened in due form.

"Mr. C. B., a candidate for initiation, being in waiting, was duly prepared, brought forward and initiated as an Entered Apprentice, he paying the usual fee.

"The Lodge of Entered Apprentices was then closed, and a Lodge of Fellow Crafts opened in due form.

"Bro. S. R., an Entered Apprentice, being in waiting, was duly prepared, brought forward and passed to the degree of a Fellow Craft, he paying the usual fee.

"The Lodge of Fellow Crafts was then closed, and a lodge of Master Masons opened in due form.

"Bro. W. Y., a Fellow Craft, being in waiting, was duly prepared, brought forward and raised to the sublime degree of a Master Mason, he paying the usual fee.

Amount received this evening, as follows:

    Petition of Mr. G. F., $5
    Fee   of Bro. C. B., 5
    do.   of Bro. S. R., 5
    do.   of Bro. W. Y., 5--Total, $20

all of which was paid over to the Treasurer.

There being no further business, the lodge was closed in due form and harmony.

    E. F----,
    Secretary.

Such is the form which has been adopted as the most convenient mode of recording the transactions of a lodge. These minutes must be read, at the close of the meeting, that the Brethren may suggest any necessary alterations or additions, and then at the beginning of the next regular meeting, that they may be confirmed, after which they should be transcribed from the rough Minute Book in which they were first entered into the permanent Record Book of the lodge.

Book Third.
The Law Of Individuals.

PASSING from the consideration of the law, which refers to Masons in their congregated masses, as the constituents of Grand and Subordinate Lodges, I next approach the discussion of the law which governs, them in their individual capacity, whether in the inception of their masonic life, as candidates for initiation, or in their gradual progress through each of the three degrees, for it will be found that a Mason, as he assumes new and additional obligations, and is presented with increased light, contracts new duties, and is invested with new prerogatives and privileges.

Chapter I.
Of the Qualifications of Candidates.

The qualifications of a candidate for initiation into the mysteries of Freemasonry, are four-fold in their character--moral, physical, intellectual and political.

The moral character is intended to secure the respectability of the Order, because, by the worthiness of its candidates, their virtuous deportment, and good reputation, will the character of the institution be judged, while the admission of irreligious libertines and contemners of the moral law would necessarily impair its dignity and honor.

The physical qualifications of a candidate contribute to the utility of the Order, because he who is deficient in any of his limbs or members, and who is not in the possession of all his natural senses and endowments, is unable to perform, with pleasure to himself or credit to the fraternity, those peculiar labors in which all should take an equal part. He thus becomes a drone in the hive, and so far impairs the usefulness of the lodge, as "a place where Freemasons assemble to work, and to instruct and improve themselves in the mysteries of their ancient science."

The intellectual qualifications refer to the security of the Order; because they require that its mysteries shall be confided only to those whose mental developments are such as to enable them properly to appreciate, and faithfully to preserve from imposition, the secrets thus entrusted to them. It is evident, for instance, that an idiot could neither understand the hidden doctrines that might be communicated to him, nor could he so secure such portions as he might remember, in the "depository of his heart," as to prevent the designing knave from worming them out of him; for, as the wise Solomon has said, "a fool's mouth is his destruction, and his lips are the snare of his soul."

The political qualifications are intended to maintain the independence of the Order; because its obligations and privileges are thus confided only to those who, from their position in society, are capable of obeying the one, and of exercising the other without the danger of let or hindrance from superior authority.

Of the moral, physical and political qualifications of a candidate there can be no doubt, as they are distinctly laid down in the ancient charges and constitutions. The intellectual are not so readily decided.

These four-fold qualifications may be briefly summed up in the following axioms.

Morally, the candidate must be a man of irreproachable conduct, a believer in the existence of God, and living "under the tongue of good report."

Physically, he must be a man of at least twenty-one years of age, upright in body, with the senses of a man, not deformed or dismembered, but with hale and entire limbs as a *man* ought to be.

Intellectually, he must be a man in the full possession of his intellects, not so young that his mind shall not have been formed, nor so old that it shall have fallen into dotage; neither a fool, an idiot, nor a madman; and with so much education as to enable him to avail himself of the teachings of Masonry, and to cultivate at his leisure a knowledge of the principles and doctrines of our royal art.

Politically, he must be in the unrestrained enjoyment of his civil and personal liberty, and this, too, by the birthright of inheritance, and not by its subsequent acquisition, in consequence of his release from hereditary bondage.

The lodge which strictly demands these qualifications of its candidates may have fewer members than one less strict, but it will undoubtedly have better ones.

But the importance of the subject demands for each class of

the qualifications a separate section, and a more extended consideration.

Section I.
Of the Moral Qualifications of Candidates.

The old charges state, that "a Mason is obliged by his tenure to obey the moral law." It is scarcely necessary to say, that the phrase, "moral law," is a technical expression of theology, and refers to the Ten Commandments, which are so called, because they define the regulations necessary for the government of the morals and manners of men. The habitual violation of any one of these commands would seem, according to the spirit of the Ancient Constitutions, to disqualify a candidate for Masonry.

The same charges go on to say, in relation to the religious character of a Mason, that he should not be "a stupid atheist, nor an irreligious libertine." A denier of the existence of a Supreme Architect of the Universe cannot, of course, be obligated as a Mason, and, accordingly, there is no landmark more certain than that which excludes every atheist from the Order.

The word "libertine" has, at this day, a meaning very different from what it bore when the old charges were compiled. It then signified what we now call a "free-thinker," or disbeliever in the divine revelation of the Scriptures. This rule would therefore greatly abridge the universality and tolerance of the Institution, were it not for the following qualifying clause in the same instrument:--

"Though in ancient times Masons were charged in every country to be of the religion of that country or nation, whatever it was, yet it is now thought more expedient only to oblige them to that religion in which all men agree, leaving their particular opinions to themselves; that is, to be good men and true, or men of honor and honesty, by whatever denominations or persuasions they may be distinguished."

The construction now given universally to the religious qualification of a candidate, is simply that he shall have a belief in the existence and superintending control of a Supreme Being.

These old charges from which we derive the whole of our doctrine as to the moral qualifications of a candidate, further prescribe as to the political relations of a Mason, that he is to be "a peaceable subject to the civil powers, wherever he resides or works, and is never to be concerned in plots and conspiracies against the peace and welfare of the nation, nor to behave himself undutifully to inferior magistrates. He is cheerfully to conform to every lawful authority; to uphold on every occasion the interest of the community, and zealously promote the prosperity of his own country."

Such being the characteristics of a true Mason, the candidate who desires to obtain that title, must show his claim to the possession of these virtues; and hence the same charges declare, in reference to these moral qualifications, that "The persons made Masons, or admitted members of a lodge, must be good and true men--no immoral or scandalous men, but of good report."

Section II.
Of the Physical Qualifications of Candidates.

The physical qualifications of a candidate refer to his sex, his age, and the condition of his limbs.

The first and most important requisite of a candidate is, that he shall be "*a man*." No woman can be made a Mason. This land-mark is so indisputable, that it would be wholly superfluous to adduce any arguments or authority in its support.

As to age, the old charges prescribe the rule, that the candi-date must be "of mature and discreet age." But what is the precise period when one is supposed to have arrived at this maturity and discretion, cannot be inferred from any uniform practice of the craft in different countries. The provisions of the civil law, which make twenty-one the age of maturity, have, however, been gen-erally followed. In this country the regulation is general, that the candidate must be twenty-one years of age. Such, too, was the regulation adopted by the General Assembly, which met on the 27th Dec., 1663, and which prescribed that "no person shall be accepted unless he be twenty-one years old or more.[55]" In Prussia, the candidate is required to be twenty-five; in England, twenty-one[56], "unless by dispensation from the Grand Master, or Provin-cial Grand Master;" in Ireland, twenty-one, except "by dispen-sation from the Grand Master, or the Grand Lodge;" in France, twenty-one, unless the candidate be the son of a Mason who has

---

55   Oliver's Preston, p. 163, note (U.M.L., vol. iii., p. 135).
56   Such is the provision in the modern constitutions of England, but the 4th of the 39 Regulations required the candidate to be at least twenty-five.

rendered important service to the craft, with the consent of his parent or guardian, or a young man who has served six months with his corps in the army--such persons may be initiated at eighteen; in Switzerland, the age of qualification is fixed at twenty-one, and in Frankfort-on-Mayn, at twenty. In this country, as I have already observed, the regulation of 1663 is rigidly enforced, and no candidate, who has not arrived at the age of twenty-one, can be initiated.

Our ritual excludes "an old man in his dotage" equally with a "young man under age." But as dotage signifies imbecility of mind, this subject will be more properly considered under the head of intellectual qualifications.

The physical qualifications, which refer to the condition of the candidate's body and limbs, have given rise, within a few years past, to a great amount of discussion and much variety of opinion. The regulation contained in the old charges of 1721, which requires the candidate to be "a perfect youth," has in some jurisdictions been rigidly enforced to the very letter of the law, while in others it has been so completely explained away as to mean anything or nothing. Thus, in South Carolina, where the rule is rigid, the candidate is required to be neither deformed nor dismembered, but of hale and entire limbs, as a man ought to be, while in Maine, a deformed person may be admitted, provided "the deformity is not such as to prevent him from being instructed in the arts and mysteries of Freemasonry."

The first written law which we find on this subject is that which was enacted by the General Assembly held in 1663, under the Grand Mastership of the Earl of St. Albans, and which declares "that no person shall hereafter be accepted a Freemason but such as are of *able* body.[57]"

Twenty years after, in the reign of James II., or about the year 1683, it seems to have been found necessary, more exactly to define the meaning of this expression, "of able body," and accordingly we find, among the charges ordered to be read to a Master on his installation, the following regulation:

"Thirdly, that he that be made be able in all degrees; that is, free-born, of a good kindred, true, and no bondsman, and that he have his right limbs as a man ought to have.[58]"

The old charges, published in the original Book of Constitutions in 1723, contain the following regulation:

"No Master should take an Apprentice, unless he be a perfect youth having no maim or defect that may render him uncapable of learning the art."

Notwithstanding the positive demand for *perfection*, and the positive and explicit declaration that he must have *no maim or defect*, the remainder of the sentence has, within a few years past, by some Grand Lodges, been considered as a qualifying clause, which would permit the admission of candidates whose physical defects did not exceed a particular point. But, in perfection, there can be no degrees of comparison, and he who is required to be perfect, is required to be so without modification or diminution. That which is *perfect* is complete in all its parts, and, by a deficiency in any portion of its constituent materials, it becomes not less perfect, (which expression would be a solecism in grammar,) but at once by the deficiency ceases to be perfect at all--it then becomes imperfect. In the interpretation of a law, "words,"

---

57   See these regulations in Preston, p. 162, Oliver's ed. (U.M.L., vol. iii., p. 135).
58   Oliver's Preston, p. 72, (U.M.L., vol. iii., p. 59).

says Blackstone, "are generally to be understood in their usual and most known signification," and then "perfect" would mean, "complete, entire, neither defective nor redundant." But another source of interpretation is, the "comparison of a law with other laws, that are made by the same legislator, that have some affinity with the subject, or that expressly relate to the same point.[59]" Applying this law of the jurists, we shall have no difficulty in arriving at the true signification of the word "perfect," if we refer to the regulation of 1683, of which the clause in question appears to have been an exposition. Now, the regulation of 1683 says, in explicit terms, that the candidate must "*have his right limbs as a man ought to have*." Comparing the one law with the other, there can be no doubt that the requisition of Masonry is and always has been, that admission could only be granted to him who was neither deformed nor dismembered, but of hale and entire limbs as a man should be.

But another, and, as Blackstone terms it, "the most universal and effectual way of discovering the true meaning of a law" is, to consider "the reason and spirit of it, or the cause which moved the legislator to enact it." Now, we must look for the origin of the law requiring physical perfection, not to the formerly operative character of the institution, (for there never was a time when it was not speculative as well as operative,) but to its symbolic nature. In the ancient temple, every stone was required to be *perfect*, for a perfect stone was the symbol of truth. In our mystic association, every Mason represents a stone in that spiritual temple, "that house not made with hands, eternal in the heavens," of which the temple of Solomon was the type. Hence it is required

59   Blackstone, Com. I., Introd., Sec. 2.

that he should present himself, like the perfect stone in the material temple, a perfect man in the spiritual building. "The symbolic relation of each member of the Order to its mystic temple, forbids the idea," says Bro. W.S. Rockwell, of Georgia[60], "that its constituent portions, its living stones, should be less perfect or less a type of their great original, than the immaculate material which formed the earthly dwelling place of the God of their adoration." If, then, as I presume it will be readily conceded, by all except those who erroneously suppose the institution to have been once wholly operative and afterwards wholly speculative, perfection is required in a candidate, not for the physical reason that he may be enabled to give the necessary signs of recognition, but because the defect would destroy the symbolism of that perfect stone which every Mason is supposed to represent in the spiritual temple, we thus arrive at a knowledge of the causes which moved the legislators of Masonry to enact the law, and we see at once, and without doubt, that the words *perfect youth* are to be taken in an unqualified sense, as signifying one who has "his right limbs as a man ought to have.[61]"

It is, however, but fair to state that the remaining clause of the old charge, which asserts that the candidate must have no maim or defect that may render him incapable of learning the art, has been supposed to intend a modification of the word "perfect," and to permit the admission of one whose maim or defect was not of such a nature as to prevent his learning the art of Mason-

---

60   In an able report on this subject, in the proceedings of the Grand Lodge of Georgia for 1852. In accordance with the views there expressed, Bro. Rockwell decided officially, as District Deputy Grand Master, in 1851, that a man who had lost one eye was not admissible.

61   Potter, 184.

ry. But I would respectfully suggest that a criticism of this kind is based upon a mistaken view of the import of the words. The sentence is not that the candidate must have no such maim or defect as might, by possibility, prevent him from learning the art; though this is the interpretation given by those who are in favor of admitting slightly maimed candidates. It is, on the contrary, so worded as to give a consequential meaning to the word "*that*." He must have no maim or defect *that* may render him incapable; that is, *because*, by having such maim or defect, he would be rendered incapable of acquiring our art.

In the Ahiman Rezon published by Laurence Dermott in 1764, and adopted for the government of the Grand Lodge of Ancient York Masons in England, and many of the Provincial Grand and subordinate lodges of America, the regulation is laid down that candidates must be "men of good report, free-born, of mature age, not deformed nor dismembered at the time of their making, and no woman or eunuch." It is true that at the present day this book possesses no legal authority among the craft; but I quote it, to show what was the interpretation given to the ancient law by a large portion, perhaps a majority, of the English and American Masons in the middle of the eighteenth century.

A similar interpretation seems at all times to have been given by the Grand Lodges of the United States, with the exception of some, who, within a few years past, have begun to adopt a more latitudinarian construction.

In Pennsylvania it was declared, in 1783, that candidates are not to be "deformed or dismembered at the time of their making."

In South Carolina the book of Constitutions, first published in 1807, requires that "every person desiring admission must be upright in body, not deformed or dismembered at the time of making, but of hale and entire limbs, as a man ought to be."

In the "Ahiman Rezon and Masonic Ritual," published by order of the Grand Lodge of North Carolina and Tennessee, in the year 1805, candidates are required to be "hale and sound, not deformed or dismembered at the time of their making.[62]"

Maryland, in 1826, sanctioned the Ahiman Rezon of Cole, which declares the law in precisely the words of South Carolina, already quoted.

In 1823, the Grand Lodge of Missouri unanimously adopted a report, which declared that all were to be refused admission who were not "sound in mind and *all their members*," and she adopted a resolution asserting that "the Grand Lodge cannot grant a letter or dispensation to a subordinate lodge working under its jurisdiction, to initiate any person maimed, disabled, or wanting the qualifications establishing by ancient usage.[63]"

But it is unnecessary to multiply instances. There never seems to have been any deviation from the principle that required absolute physical perfection, until, within a few years, the spirit of expediency[64] has induced some Grand Lodges to propose a modified

---

62   Page 18. In December, 1851, the Committee of Correspondence of North Carolina, unregardful of the rigid rule of their predecessors, decided that maimed candidates might be initiated, "provided their loss or infirmity will not prevent them from making full proficiency in Masonry."

63   Proceedings of the G.L. of Mo. for 1823, p. 5. The report and resolution were on the petitions of two candidates to be initiated, one with only one arm, and the other much deformed in his legs.

64   When the spirit of expediency once begins, we know not where it will stop. Thus a blind man has been initiated in Mississippi, and a one-armed one in Kentucky; and in France a few years since, the degrees were conferred by sign-language on a deaf mute!

construction of the law, and to admit those whose maims or deformities were not such as to prevent them from complying with the ceremonial of initiation. Still, a large number of the Grand Lodges have stood fast by the ancient landmark, and it is yet to be hoped that all will return to their first allegiance. The subject is an important one, and, therefore, a few of the more recent authorities, in behalf of the old law may with advantage be cited.

"We have examined carefully the arguments 'pro and con,' that have accompanied the proceedings of the several Grand Lodges, submitted to us, and the conviction has been forced upon our minds, even against our wills, that we depart from the ancient landmarks and usages of Masonry, whenever we admit an individual wanting in one of the human senses, or who is in any particular maimed or deformed."-- Committee of Correspondence G. Lodge of Georgia, 1848, *page* 36.

"The rationale of the law, excluding persons physically imperfect and deformed, lies deeper and is more ancient than the source ascribed to it[65]. It is grounded on a principle recognized in the earliest ages of the world; and will be found identical with that which obtained among the ancient Jews. In this respect the Levitical law was the same as the masonic, which would not allow any 'to go in unto the vail' who had a blemish--a blind man, or a lame, or a man that was broken-footed, or broken-handed, or a dwarf, &c....

"The learned and studious Freemasonic antiquary can satisfactorily explain the metaphysics of this requisition in our Book

---

65   Namely, the incorrectly presumed operative origin of the Order. The whole of this report, which is from the venerable Giles F. Yates, contains an able and unanswerable defense of the ancient law in opposition to any qualification.

of Constitutions. For the true and faithful Brother it sufficeth to know that such a requisition exists. He will prize it the more because of its antiquity.... No man can in perfection be 'made a Brother,' no man can truly 'learn our mysteries,' and practice them, or 'do the work of a Freemason,' if he is not a *man* with body free from maim, defect and deformity."--Report of a Special Committee of the Grand Lodge of New York, in 1848[66].

"The records of this Grand Lodge may be confidently appealed to, for proofs of her repeated refusal to permit maimed persons to be initiated, and not simply on the ground that ancient usage forbids it, but because the fundamental constitution of the Order--the ancient charges--forbid it."--Committee of Correspondence of New York, for 1848, p. 70.

"The lodges subordinate to this Grand Lodge are hereby required, in the initiation of applicants for Masonry, to adhere to the ancient law (as laid down in our printed books), which says he shall be of *entire limbs*"--Resolution of the G.L. of Maryland, November, 1848.

"I received from the lodge at Ashley a petition to initiate into our Order a gentleman of high respectability, who, unfortunately, has been maimed. I refused my assent.... I have also refused a similar request from the lodge of which I am a member. The fact that the most distinguished masonic body on earth has recently removed one of the landmarks, should teach *us* to be careful how we touch those ancient boundaries."--Address of the Grand Master of New Jersey in 1849.

"The Grand Lodge of Florida adopted such a provision in her constitution, [the qualifying clause permitting the initiation of a

66   See proceedings of New York, 1848, pp. 36, 37.

maimed person, if his deformity was not such as to prevent his instruction], but more mature reflection, and more light reflected from our sister Grand Lodges, caused it to be stricken from our constitution."--Address of Gov. Tho. Brown, Grand Master of Florida in 1849.

"As to the physical qualifications, the Ahiman Rezon leaves no doubt on the subject, but expressly declares, that every applicant for initiation must be a man, free-born, of lawful age, in the perfect enjoyment of his senses, hale, and sound, and not deformed or dismembered; this is one of the ancient landmarks of the Order, which it is in the power of no body of men to change. A man having but one arm, or one leg, or who is in anyway deprived of his due proportion of limbs and members, is as incapable of initiation as a woman."--*Encyclical Letter of the Grand Lodge of South Carolina to its subordinates in* 1849.

Impressed, then, by the weight of these authorities, which it would be easy, but is unnecessary, to multiply--guided by a reference to the symbolic and speculative (not operative) reason of the law--and governed by the express words of the regulation of 1683--I am constrained to believe that the spirit as well as the letter of our ancient landmarks require that a candidate for admission should be perfect in all his parts, that is, neither redundant nor deficient, neither deformed nor dismembered, but of hale and entire limbs, as a man ought to be.

Section III.
Of the Intellectual Qualifications of Candidates.

The Old Charges and Ancient Constitutions are not as explicit in relation to the intellectual as to the moral and physical qualifications of candidates, and, therefore, in coming to a decision on this subject, we are compelled to draw our conclusions from analogy, from common sense, and from the peculiar character of the institution. The question that here suggests itself on this subject is, what particular amount of human learning is required as a constitutional qualification for initiation?

During a careful examination of every ancient document to which I have had access, I have met with no positive enactment forbidding the admission of uneducated persons, even of those who can neither read nor write. The unwritten, as well as the written laws of the Order, require that the candidate shall be neither a *fool nor an idiot*, but that he shall possess a discreet judgment, and be in the enjoyment of all the senses of a man. But one who is unable to subscribe his name, or to read it when written, might still very easily prove himself to be within the requirements of this regulation. The Constitutions of England, formed since the union of the two Grand Lodges in 1813, are certainly explicit enough on this subject. They require even more than a bare knowledge of reading and writing, for, in describing the qualifications of a candidate, they say:

"He should be a lover of the liberal arts and sciences, and have made some progress in one or other of them; and he must, previous to his initiation, subscribe his name at full length, to a declaration of the following import," etc. And in a note to this regulation, it is said, "Any individual who cannot write is, consequently, ineligible to be admitted into the Order." If this authority were universal in its character, there would be no necessity for a further discussion of the subject. But the modern constitutions of the Grand Lodge of England are only of force within its own jurisdiction, and we are therefore again compelled to resort to a mode of reasoning for the proper deduction of our conclusions on this subject.

It is undoubtedly true that in the early period of the world, when Freemasonry took its origin, the arts of reading and writing were not so generally disseminated among all classes of the community as they now are, when the blessings of a common education can be readily and cheaply obtained. And it may, therefore, be supposed that among our ancient Brethren there were many who could neither read nor write. But after all, this is a mere assumption, which, although it may be based on probability, has no direct evidence for its support. And, on the other hand, we see throughout all our ancient regulations, that a marked distinction was made by our rulers between the Freemason and the Mason who was not free; as, for instance, in the conclusion of the fifth chapter of the Ancient Charges, where it is said: "No laborer shall be employed in the common work of Masonry, nor shall Freemasons work with those who are not free, without an urgent necessity." And this would seem to indicate a higher estimation by the fraternity of their own character, which might be derived from their greater attainments in knowledge. That in those days the ordinary operative masons could neither read nor write, is a fact established by history. But it does not follow that the Freemasons, who were a separate society of craftsmen, were in the same unhappy category; it is even probable, that the fact that they were not so, but that they were, in comparison with the unaccepted masons, educated men, may have been the reason of the distinction made between these two classes of workmen.

But further, all the teachings of Freemasonry are delivered on the assumption that the recipients are men of some education, with the means of improving their minds and increasing their knowledge. Even the Entered Apprentice is reminded, by the rough and perfect ashlars, of the importance and necessity of a virtuous education, in fitting him for the discharge of his duties. To the Fellow Craft, the study of the liberal arts and sciences is earnestly recommended; and indeed, that sacred hieroglyphic, the knowledge of whose occult signification constitutes the most solemn part of his instruction, presupposes an acquaintance at least with the art of reading. And the Master Mason is expressly told in the explanation of the forty-seventh problem of Euclid, as one of the symbols of the third degree, that it was introduced into Masonry to teach the Brethren the value of the arts and sciences, and that the Mason, like the discoverer of the problem, our ancient Brother Pythagoras, should be a diligent cultivator of learning. Our lectures, too, abound in allusions which none but a person of some cultivation of mind could understand or appreciate, and to address them, or any portion of our charges which refer to the improvement of the intellect and the augmentation of knowledge, to persons who can neither read nor write, would be, it seems to us, a mockery unworthy of the sacred character of our institution.

From these facts and this method of reasoning, I deduce the conclusion that the framers of Masonry, in its present organization as a speculative institution, must have intended to admit none into its fraternity whose minds had not received some preliminary cultivation, and I am, therefore, clearly of opinion, that a person who cannot read and write is not legally qualified for admission.

As to the inexpediency of receiving such candidates, there can be no question or doubt. If Masonry be, as its disciples claim for it, a scientific institution, whose great object is to improve the understanding and to enlarge and adorn the mind, whose character cannot be appreciated, and whose lessons of symbolic wisdom cannot be acquired, without much studious application, how preposterous would it be to place, among its disciples, one who had lived to adult years, without having known the necessity or felt the ambition for a knowledge of the alphabet of his mother tongue? Such a man could make no advancement in the art of Masonry; and while he would confer no substantial advantage on the institution, he would, by his manifest incapacity and ignorance, detract, in the eyes of strangers, from its honor and dignity as an intellectual society.

Idiots and madmen are excluded from admission into the Order, for the evident reason that the former from an absence, and the latter from a perversion of the intellectual faculties, are incapable of comprehending the objects, or of assuming the responsibilities and obligations of the institution.

A question here suggests itself whether a person of present sound mind, but who had formerly been deranged, can legally be initiated. The answer to this question turns on the fact of his having perfectly recovered. If the present sanity of the applicant is merely a lucid interval, which physicians know to be sometimes vouched to lunatics, with the absolute certainty, or at best, the strong probability, of an eventual return to a state of mental derangement, he is not, of course, qualified for initiation. But if there has been a real and durable recovery (of which a physician will be a competent judge), then there can be no possible objection to his admission, if otherwise eligible. We are not to look to what the candidate once was, but to what he now is.

Dotage, or the mental imbecility produced by excessive old age, is also a disqualification for admission. Distinguished as it is by puerile desires and pursuits, by a failure of the memory, a deficiency of the judgment, and a general obliteration of the mental powers, its external signs are easily appreciated, and furnish at once abundant reason why, like idiots and madmen, the superannuated dotard is unfit to be the recipient of our mystic instructions.

Section IV.
Of the Political Qualifications of Candidates.

The Constitutions of Masonry require, as the only qualification referring to the political condition of the candidate, or his position in society, that he shall be free-born. The slave, or even the man born in servitude--though he may, subsequently, have obtained his liberty--is excluded by the ancient regulations from initiation. The non-admission of a slave seems to have been founded upon the best of reasons; because, as Freemasonry involves a solemn contract, no one can legally bind himself to its performance who is not a free agent and the master of his own actions. That the restriction is extended to those who were originally in a servile condition, but who may have since acquired their liberty, seems to depend on the principle that birth, in a servile condition, is accompanied by a degradation of mind and abasement of spirit, which no subsequent disenthralment can so completely efface as to render the party qualified to perform his duties, as a Mason, with that "freedom, fervency, and zeal," which are said to have distinguished our ancient Brethren. "Children," says Oliver, "cannot inherit a free and noble spirit except they be born of a free woman."

The same usage existed in the spurious Freemasonry or the Mysteries of the ancient world. There, no slave, or men born in slavery, could be initiated; because, the prerequisites imperatively demanded that the candidate should not only be a man of irreproachable manners, but also a free-born denizen of the country in which the mysteries were celebrated.

Some masonic writers have thought that, in this regulation in relation to free birth, some allusion is intended, both in the Mysteries and in Freemasonry, to the relative conditions and characters of Isaac and Ishmael. The former--the accepted one, to whom the promise was given--was the son of a free woman, and the latter, who was cast forth to have "his hand against every man, and every man's hand against him," was the child of a slave. Wherefore, we read that Sarah demanded of Abraham, "Cast out this bondwoman and her son; for the son of the bondwoman shall not be heir with my son." Dr. Oliver, in speaking of the grand festival with which Abraham celebrated the weaning of Isaac, says, that he "had not paid the same compliment at the weaning of Ishmael, because he was the son of a bondwoman, and, consequently, could not be admitted to participate in the Freemasonry of his father, which could only be conferred on free men born of free women." The ancient Greeks were of the same opinion; for they used the word [Greek: douloprepeia] or, "slave manners," to designate any very great impropriety of manners.

The Grand Lodge of England extends this doctrine, that Masons should be free in all their thoughts and actions, so far, that it will not permit the initiation of a candidate who is only temporarily deprived of his liberty, or even in a place of confinement. In the year 1782, the Master of the Royal Military Lodge, at Woolwich, being confined, most probably for debt, in the King's Bench prison, at London, the lodge, which was itinerant in its character, and allowed to move from place to place with its regiment, adjourned, with its warrant of constitution, to the Master in prison, where several Masons were made. The Grand Lodge, being informed of the circumstances, immediately summoned the Master and Wardens of the lodge "to answer for their conduct in making Masons in the King's Bench prison," and, at the same time, adopted a resolution, affirming that "it is inconsistent with the principles of Freemasonry for any Freemason's lodge to be held, for the purposes of making, passing, or raising Masons, in any prison or place of confinement."

Section V.
Of the Petition of Candidates for
Admission, and the Action thereon.

The application of a candidate to a lodge, for initiation, is called a "petition." This petition should always be in writing, and generally contains a statement of the petitioner's age, occupation, and place of residence, and a declaration of the motives which have prompted the application, which ought to be "a favorable opinion conceived of the institution and a desire of knowledge.[67]"

67   Such is the formula prescribed by the Constitutions of England as well as all the Moni-

This petition must be recommended by at least two members of the lodge.

The petition must be read at a stated or regular communication of the lodge, and referred to a committee of three members for an investigation of the qualifications and character of the candidate. The committee having made the necessary inquiries, will report the result at the next regular communication and not sooner.

The authority for this deliberate mode of proceeding is to be found in the fifth of the 39 General Regulations, which is in these words:

"No man can be made or admitted a member of a particular lodge, without previous notice one month before given to the said lodge, in order to make due inquiry into the reputation and capacity of the candidate; unless by dispensation aforesaid."

The last clause in this article provides for the only way in which this probation of a month can be avoided, and that is when the Grand Master, for reasons satisfactory to himself, being such as will constitute what is called (sometimes improperly) a case of emergency, shall issue a dispensation permitting the lodge to proceed forthwith to the election.

But where this dispensation has not been issued, the committee should proceed diligently and faithfully to the discharge of their responsible duty. They must inquire into the moral, physical, intellectual and political qualifications of the candidate, and make their report in accordance with the result of their investigations.

The report cannot be made at a special communication, but

tors in this country.

must always be presented at a regular one. The necessity of such a rule is obvious. As the Master can at any time within his discretion convene a special meeting of his lodge, it is evident that a presiding officer, if actuated by an improper desire to intrude an unworthy and unpopular applicant upon the craft, might easily avail himself for that purpose of an occasion when the lodge being called for some other purpose, the attendance of the members was small, and causing a ballot to be taken, succeed in electing a candidate, who would, at a regular meeting, have been blackballed by some of those who were absent from the special communication.

This regulation is promulgated by the Grand Lodge of England, in the following words: "No person shall be made a Mason without a regular proposition at one lodge and a ballot at the next regular stated lodge;" it appears to have been almost universally adopted in similar language by the Grand Lodges of this country; and, if the exact words of the law are wanting in any of the Constitutions, the general usage of the craft has furnished an equivalent authority for the regulation.

If the report of the committee is unfavorable, the candidate should be considered as rejected, without any reference to a ballot. This rule is also founded in reason. If the committee, after a due inquiry into the character of the applicant, find the result so disadvantageous to him as to induce them to make an unfavorable report on his application, it is to be presumed that on a ballot they would vote against his admission, and as their votes alone would be sufficient to reject him, it is held unnecessary to resort in such a case to the supererogatory ordeal of the ballot. It would, indeed, be an anomalous proceeding, and one which would reflect great discredit on the motives and conduct of a committee of inquiry, were its members first to report against the reception of a candidate, and then, immediately afterwards, to vote in favor of his petition. The lodges will not suppose, for the honor of their committees, that such a proceeding will take place, and accordingly the unfavorable report of the committee is always to be considered as a rejection.

Another reason for this regulation seems to be this. The fifth General Regulation declares that no Lodge should ever make a Mason without "due inquiry" into his character, and as the duty of making this inquiry is entrusted to a competent committee, when that committee has reported that the applicant is unworthy to be made a Mason, it would certainly appear to militate against the spirit, if not the letter, of the regulation, for the lodge, notwithstanding this report, to enter into a ballot on the petition.

But should the committee of investigation report favorably, the lodge will then proceed to a ballot for the candidate; but, as this forms a separate and important step in the process of "making Masons," I shall make it the subject of a distinct section.

Section VI.
Of Balloting for Candidates.

The Thirty-nine Regulations do not explicitly prescribe the ballot-box as the proper mode of testing the opinion of the lodge on the merits of a petition for initiation. The sixth regulation simply says that the consent of the members is to be "formally asked by the Master; and they are to signify their assent or dissent *in their own prudent way* either virtually or in form, but with unanimity." Almost universal usage has, however, sanctioned the ballot box and the use of black and white balls as the proper mode of obtaining the opinion of the members.

From the responsibility of expressing this opinion, and of admitting a candidate into the fraternity or of repulsing him from it, no Mason is permitted to shrink. In balloting on a petition, therefore, every member of the Lodge is expected to vote; nor can he be excused from the discharge of this important duty, except by the unanimous consent of his Brethren. All the members must, therefore, come up to the performance of this trust with firmness, candor, and a full determination to do what is right--to allow no personal timidity to forbid the deposit of a black ball, if the applicant is unworthy, and no illiberal prejudices to prevent the deposition of a white one, if the character and qualifications of the candidate are unobjectionable. And in all cases where a member himself has no personal or acquired knowledge of these qualifications, he should rely upon and be governed by the recommendation of his Brethren of the Committee of Investigation, who he has no right to suppose would make a favorable report on the petition of an unworthy applicant[68].

The great object of the ballot is, to secure the independence of the voter; and, for this purpose, its secrecy should be inviolate. And this secrecy of the ballot gives rise to a particular rule which necessarily flows out of it.

No Mason can be called to an account for the vote which he has deposited. The very secrecy of the ballot is intended to secure the independence and irresponsibility to the lodge of the voter. And, although it is undoubtedly a crime for a member to vote

68   See Mackey's Lexicon of Freemasonry, 3d Edit., art, _Ballot_.

against the petition of an applicant on account of private pique or personal prejudice, still the lodge has no right to judge that such motives alone actuated him. The motives of men, unless divulged by themselves, can be known only to God; "and if," as Wayland says, "from any circumstances we are led to entertain any doubts of the motives of men, we are bound to retain these doubts within our own bosoms." Hence, no judicial notice can be or ought to be taken by a lodge of a vote cast by a member, on the ground of his having been influenced by improper motives, because it is impossible for the lodge legally to arrive at the knowledge; in the first place, of the vote that he has given, and secondly, of the motives by which he has been controlled.

And even if a member voluntarily should divulge the nature of his vote and of his motives, it is still exceedingly questionable whether the lodge should take any notice of the act, because by so doing the independence of the ballot might be impaired. It is through a similar mode of reasoning that the Constitution of the United States provides, that the members of Congress shall not be questioned, in any other place, for any speech or debate in either House. As in this way the freedom of debate is preserved in legislative bodies, so in like manner should the freedom of the ballot be insured in lodges.

The sixth General Regulation requires unanimity in the ballot. Its language is: "but no man can be entered a Brother in any particular lodge, or admitted to be a member thereof, without the *unanimous consent of all the members of that lodge* then present when the candidate is proposed." This regulation, it will be remembered, was adopted in 1721. But in the "New Regulations," adopted in 1754, and which are declared to have been enacted "only for amending or explaining the Old Regulations for the good of Masonry, without breaking in upon the ancient rules of the fraternity, still preserving the old landmarks," it is said: "but it was found inconvenient to insist upon unanimity in several cases; and, therefore, the Grand Masters have allowed the lodges to admit a member, if not above three black balls are against him; though some lodges desire no such allowance.[69]"

The Grand Lodge of England still acts under this new regulation, and extends the number of black balls which will reject to three, though it permits its subordinates, if they desire it, to require unanimity. But nearly all the Grand Lodges of this country have adhered to the old regulation, which is undoubtedly the better one, and by special enactment have made the unanimous consent of all the Brethren present necessary to the election of a candidate.

Another question here suggests itself. Can a member, who by the bye-laws of his lodge is disqualified from the exercise of his other franchises as a member, in consequence of being in arrears beyond a certain amount, be prevented from depositing his ballot on the application of a candidate? That by such a bye-law he may be disfranchised of his vote in electing officers, or of the right to hold office, will be freely admitted. But the words of the old regulation seem expressly, and without equivocation, to require that *every member present* shall vote. The candidate shall only be admitted "by the unanimous consent of all the members of that lodge then present when the candidate is proposed." This right of the members to elect or reject their candidates is subsequently called "an inherent privilege," which is not subject to a dispen-

---

69   Book of Constitutions. Edit. 1755, p. 312.

sation. The words are explicit, and the right appears to be one guaranteed to every member so long as he continues a member, and of which no bye-law can divest him as long as the paramount authority of the Thirty-nine General Regulations is admitted. I should say, then, that every member of a lodge present at balloting for a candidate has a right to deposit his vote; and not only a right, but a duty which he is to be compelled to perform; since, without the unanimous consent of all present, there can be no election.

Our written laws are altogether silent as to the peculiar ceremonies which are to accompany the act of balloting, which has therefore been generally directed by the local usage of different jurisdictions. Uniformity, however, in this, as in all other ritual observances, is to be commended, and I shall accordingly here describe the method which I have myself preferred and practised in balloting for candidates, and which is the custom adopted in the jurisdiction of South Carolina[70].

The committee of investigation having reported favorably, the Master of the lodge directs the Senior Deacon to prepare the ballot box. The mode in which this is accomplished is as follows:--The Senior Deacon takes the ballot box, and, opening it, places all the white and black balls indiscriminately in one compartment, leaving the other entirely empty. He then proceeds with the box to the Junior and Senior Wardens, who satisfy themselves by an inspection that no ball has been left in the compartment in which the votes are to be deposited. I remark here, in passing, that the box, in this and the other instance to be referred to hereafter, is presented to the inferior officer first, and then to his

70   See Mackey's Lexicon of Freemasonry, 3d Edit., art. _Ballot_

superior, that the examination and decision of the former may be substantiated and confirmed by the higher authority of the latter. Let it, indeed, be remembered, that in all such cases the usage of masonic *circumambulation* is to be observed, and that, therefore, we must first pass the Junior's station before we can get to that of the Senior Warden.

These officers having thus satisfied themselves that the box is in a proper condition for the reception of the ballots, it is then placed upon the altar by the Senior Deacon, who retires to his seat. The Master then directs the Secretary to call the roll, which is done by commencing with the Worshipful Master, and proceeding through all the officers down to the youngest member. As a matter of convenience, the Secretary generally votes the last of those in the room, and then, if the Tiler is a member of the lodge, he is called in, while the Junior Deacon tiles for him, and the name of the applicant having been told him, he is directed to deposit his ballot, which he does, and then retires.

As the name of each officer and member is called he approaches the altar, and having made the proper masonic salutation to the Chair, he deposits his ballot and retires to his seat. The roll should be called slowly, so that at no time should there be more than one person present at the box; for, the great object of the ballot being secrecy, no Brother should be permitted so near the member voting as to distinguish the color of the ball he deposits.

The box is placed on the altar, and the ballot is deposited with the solemnity of a masonic salutation, that the voters may be duly impressed with the sacred and responsible nature of the duty they are called on to discharge. The system of voting thus described, is, therefore, far better on this account than the one sometimes adopted in lodges, of handing round the box for the members to deposit their ballots from their seats

The Master having inquired of the Wardens if all have voted, then orders the Senior Deacon to "take charge of the ballot box." That officer accordingly repairs to the altar, and taking possession of the box, carries it, as before, to the Junior Warden, who examines the ballot, and reports, if all the balls are white, that "the box is clear in the South," or, if there is one or more black balls, that "the box is foul in the South." The Deacon then carries it to the Senior Warden, and afterwards to the Master, who, of course, make the same report, according to the circumstances, with the necessary verbal variation of "West" and "East."

If the box is *clear*--that is, if all the ballots are white--the Master then announces that the applicant has been duly elected, and the Secretary makes a record of the fact.

But if the box is declared to be *foul*, the Master inspects the number of black balls; if he finds two, he declares the candidate to be rejected; if only one, he so states the fact to the lodge, and orders the Senior Deacon again to prepare the ballot box, and a second ballot is taken in the same way. This is done lest a black ball might have been inadvertently voted on the first ballot. If, on the second scrutiny, one black ball is again found, the fact is announced by the Master, who orders the election to lie over until the next stated meeting, and requests the Brother who deposited the black ball to call upon him and state his reasons. At the next stated meeting the Master announces these reasons to the lodge, if any have been made known to him, concealing, of course, the name of the objecting Brother. At this time the validity or truth of the objections may be discussed, and the friends of the applicant will have an opportunity of offering any defense or explanation.

The ballot is then taken a third time, and the result, whatever it may be, is final. As I have already observed, in most of the lodges of this country, a reappearance of the one black ball will amount to a rejection. In those lodges which do not require unanimity, it will, of course, be necessary that the requisite number of black balls must be deposited on this third ballot to insure a rejection. But if, on inspection, the box is found to be "clear," or without a black ball, the candidate is, of course, declared to be elected. In any case, the result of the third ballot is final, nor can it be set aside or reversed by the action of the Grand Master or Grand Lodge; because, by the sixth General Regulation, already so frequently cited, the members of every particular lodge are the best judges of the qualifications of their candidates; and, to use the language of the Regulation, "if a fractious member should be imposed on them, it might spoil their harmony, or hinder their freedom, or even break and disperse the lodge."

Section VII.
Of the Reconsideration of the Ballot.

There are, unfortunately, some men in our Order, governed, not by essentially bad motives, but by frail judgments and by total ignorance of the true object and design of Freemasonry, who never, under any circumstances, have recourse to the black ball, that great bulwark of Masonry, and are always more or less incensed when any more judicious Brother exercises his privilege of excluding those whom he thinks unworthy of participation in our mysteries.

I have said, that these men are not governed by motives essentially bad. This is the fact. They honestly desire the prosperity of the institution, and they would not willfully do one act which would impede that prosperity. But their judgments are weak, and their zeal is without knowledge. They do not at all understand in what the true prosperity of the Order consists, but really and conscientiously believing that its actual strength will be promoted by the increase of the number of its disciples; they look rather to the *quantity than to the quality* of the applicants who knock at the doors of our lodges.

Now a great difference in respect to the mode in which the ballot is conducted, will be found in those lodges which are free from the presence of such injudicious brethren, and others into which they have gained admittance.

In a lodge in which every member has a correct notion of the proper moral qualifications of the candidates for Masonry, and where there is a general disposition to work well with a few, rather than to work badly with many, when a ballot is ordered, each Brother, having deposited his vote, quietly and calmly waits to hear the decision of the ballot box announced by the Chair. If it is "clear," all are pleased that another citizen has been found worthy to receive a portion of the illuminating rays of Masonry. If it is "foul," each one is satisfied with the adjudication, and rejoices that, although knowing nothing himself against the candidate, some one has been present whom a more intimate acquaintance with the character of the applicant has enabled to interpose his veto, and prevent the purity of the Order from being sullied by the admission of an unworthy candidate. Here the matter ends, and the lodge proceeds to other business.

But in a lodge where one of these injudicious and over-zealous Brethren is present, how different is the scene. If the candidate is elected, he, too, rejoices; but his joy is, that the lodge has gained one more member whose annual dues and whose initiation fee will augment the amount of its revenues. If he is rejected, he is indignant that the lodge has been deprived of this pecuniary accession, and forthwith he sets to work to reverse, if possible, the decision of the ballot box, and by a volunteer defense of the rejected candidate, and violent denunciations of those who opposed him, he seeks to alarm the timid and disgust the intelligent, so that, on a *reconsideration*, they may be induced to withdraw their opposition.

The *motion for reconsideration* is, then, the means generally adopted, by such seekers after quantity, to insure the success of their efforts to bring all into our fold who seek admission, irrespective of worth or qualification. In other words, we may say, that *the motion for reconsideration is the great antagonist of the purity and security of the ballot box*. The importance, then, of the position which it thus assumes, demands a brief discussion of the time and mode in which a ballot may be reconsidered.

In the beginning of the discussion, it may be asserted, that it is competent for any brother to move a reconsideration of a ballot, or for a lodge to vote on such a motion. The ballot is a part of the work of initiating a candidate. It is the preparatory step, and is just as necessary to his legal making as the obligation or the investiture. As such, then, it is clearly entirely under the control of the Master. The Constitutions of Masonry and the Rules and Regulations of every Grand and Subordinate lodge prescribe the mode in which the ballot shall be conducted, so that the sense of the members may be taken. The Grand Lodge also requires that the Master of the lodge shall see that that exact mode of ballot shall be pursued and no other, and it will hold him responsible that there shall be no violation of the rule. If, then, the Master is satisfied that the ballot has been regularly and correctly conducted, and that no possible good, but some probable evil, would arise from its reconsideration, it is not only competent for him, but it is his solemn duty to refuse to permit any such reconsideration. A motion to that effect, it may be observed, will always be out of order, although any Brother may respectfully request the Worshipful Master to order such a reconsideration, or suggest to him its propriety or expediency.

If, however, the Master is not satisfied that the ballot is a true indication of the sense of the lodge, he may, in his own discretion, order a reconsideration. Thus there may be but one black ball;--now a single black ball may sometimes be inadvertently cast--the member voting it may have been favorably disposed towards the candidate, and yet, from the hurry and confusion of voting, or from the dimness of the light or the infirmity of his own eyes, or from some other equally natural cause, he may have selected a black ball, when he intended to have taken a white one. It is, therefore, a matter of prudence and necessary caution, that, when only one black ball appears, the Master should order a new ballot. On this second ballot, it is to be presumed that more care and vigilance will be used, and the reappearance of the black ball will then show that it was deposited designedly.

But where two or three or more black balls appear on the first ballot, such a course of reasoning is not authorized, and the Master will then be right to refuse a reconsideration. The ballot has then been regularly taken--the lodge has emphatically decided for a rejection, and any order to renew the ballot would only be an insult to those who opposed the admission of the applicant, and an indirect attempt to thrust an unwelcome intruder upon the lodge.

But although it is in the power of the Master, under the circumstances which we have described, to order a reconsideration, yet this prerogative is accompanied with certain restrictions, which it may be well to notice.

In the first place, the Master cannot order a reconsideration on any other night than that on which the original ballot was taken[71]. After the lodge is closed, the decision of the ballot is final, and there is no human authority that can reverse it. The reason of this rule is evident. If it were otherwise, an unworthy Master (for, unfortunately, all Masters are not worthy) might on any subsequent evening avail himself of the absence of those who had voted black balls, to order a reconsideration, and thus succeed in introducing an unfit and rejected candidate into the lodge, contrary to the wishes of a portion of its members.

Neither can he order a reconsideration on the same night, if any of the Brethren who voted have retired. All who expressed their opinion on the first ballot, must be present to express it on the second. The reasons for this restriction are as evident as for the former, and are of the same character.

It must be understood, that I do not here refer to those reconsiderations of the ballot which are necessary to a full understanding of the opinion of the lodge, and which have been detailed in

---

71 Except when there is but one black ball, in which case the matter lies over until the next stated meeting. See preceding Section.

the ceremonial of the mode of balloting, as it was described in the preceding Section.

It may be asked whether the Grand Master cannot, by his dispensations, permit a reconsideration. I answer emphatically, NO. The Grand Master possesses no such prerogative. There is no law in the whole jurisprudence of the institution clearer than this-- that neither the Grand Lodge nor the Grand Master can interfere with the decision of the ballot box. In Anderson's Constitutions, the law is laid down, under the head of "Duty of Members" (edition of 1755, p. 312), that in the election of candidates the Brethren "are to give their consent in their own prudent way, either virtually or in form, but with unanimity." And the regulation goes on to say: "Nor is this inherent privilege *subject to a dispensation*, because the members of a lodge are the best judges of it; and because, if a turbulent member should be imposed upon them, it might spoil their harmony, or hinder the freedom of their communications, or even break and disperse the lodge." This settles the question. A dispensation to reconsider a ballot would be an interference with the right of the members "to give their consent in their own prudent way;" it would be an infringement of an "inherent privilege," and neither the Grand Lodge nor the Grand Master can issue a dispensation for such a purpose. Every lodge must be left to manage its own elections of candidates in its own prudent way.

I conclude this section by a summary of the principles which have been discussed, and which I have endeavored to enforce by a process of reasoning which I trust may be deemed sufficiently convincing. They are briefly these:

1. It is never in order for a member to move for the reconsid-

eration of a ballot on the petition of a candidate for initiation, nor
for a lodge to entertain such a motion.

2. The Master alone can, for reasons satisfactory to himself,
order such a reconsideration.

3. The Master cannot order a reconsideration on any subsequent night, nor on the same night, after any member, who was
present and voted, has departed.

4. The Grand Master cannot grant a dispensation for a reconsideration, nor in any other way interfere with the ballot. The
same restriction applies to the Grand Lodge.

Section VIII.
Of the Renewal of Applications by Rejected Candidates.

As it is apparent from the last section that there can be no
reconsideration by a lodge of a rejected petition, the question will
naturally arise, how an error committed by a lodge, in the rejection of a worthy applicant, is to be corrected, or how such a
candidate, when once rejected, is ever to make a second trial, for
it is, of course, admitted, that circumstances may occur in which
a candidate who had been once blackballed might, on a renewal
of his petition, be found worthy of admission. He may have since
reformed and abandoned the vicious habits which caused his first
rejection, or it may have been since discovered that that rejection
was unjust. How, then, is such a candidate to make a new application?

It is a rule of universal application in Masonry, that no candidate, having been once rejected, can apply to any other lodge
for admission, except to the one which rejected him. Under this

regulation the course of a second application is as follows:

Some Grand Lodges have prescribed that, when a candidate has been rejected, it shall not be competent for him to apply within a year, six months, or some other definite period. This is altogether a local regulation--there is no such law in the Ancient Constitutions--and therefore, where the regulations of the Grand Lodge of the jurisdiction are silent upon the subject, general principles direct the following as the proper course for a rejected candidate to pursue on a second application. He must send in a new letter, recommended and vouched for as before, either by the same or other Brethren--it must be again referred to a committee--lie over for a month--and the ballot be then taken as is usual in other cases. It must be treated in all respects as an entirely new petition, altogether irrespective of the fact that the same person had ever before made an application. In this way due notice will be given to the Brethren, and all possibility of an unfair election will be avoided.

If the local regulations are silent upon the subject, the second application may be made at any time after the rejection of the first, all that is necessary being, that the second application should pass through the same ordeal and be governed by the same rules that prevail in relation to an original application.

Section IX.
Of the necessary Probation and due Proficiency
of Candidates before Advancement.

There is, perhaps, no part of the jurisprudence of Masonry which it is more necessary strictly to observe than that which relates to the advancement of candidates through the several degrees. The method which is adopted in passing Apprentices and raising Fellow Crafts--the probation which they are required to serve in each degree before advancing to a higher--and the instructions which they receive in their progress, often materially affect the estimation which is entertained of the institution by its initiates. The candidate who long remains at the porch of the temple, and lingers in the middle chamber, noting everything worthy of observation in his passage to the holy of holies, while he better understands the nature of the profession upon which he has entered, will have a more exalted opinion of its beauties and excellencies than he who has advanced, with all the rapidity that dispensations can furnish, from the lowest to the highest grades of the Order. In the former case, the design, the symbolism, the history, and the moral and philosophical bearing of each degree will be indelibly impressed upon the mind, and the appositeness of what has gone before to what is to succeed will be readily appreciated; but, in the latter, the lessons of one hour will be obliterated by those of the succeeding one; that which has been learned in one degree, will be forgotten in the next; and when all is completed, and the last instructions have been imparted, the dissatisfied neophyte will find his mind, in all that relates to Masonry, in a state of chaotic confusion. Like Cassio, he will remember "a mass of things, but nothing distinctly."

An hundred years ago it was said that "Masonry was a progressive science, and not to be attained in any degree of perfection, but by time, patience, and a considerable degree of application and industry.[72]" And it is because that due proportion of time,

---

72   Masonry founded on Scripture, a Sermon preached in 1752, by the Rev. W. Williams.

patience and application, has not been observed, that we so often see Masons indifferent to the claims of the institution, and totally unable to discern its true character. The arcana of the craft, as Dr. Harris remarks, should be gradually imparted to its members, according to their improvement.

There is no regulation of our Order more frequently repeated in our constitutions, nor one which should be more rigidly observed, than that which requires of every candidate a "suitable proficiency" in one degree, before he is permitted to pass to another. But as this regulation is too often neglected, to the manifest injury of the whole Order, as well as of the particular lodge which violates it, by the introduction of ignorant and unskillful workmen into the temple, it may be worth the labor we shall spend upon the subject, to investigate some of the authorities which support us in the declaration, that no candidate should be promoted, until, by a due probation, he has made "suitable proficiency in the preceding degree."

In one of the earliest series of regulations that have been preserved--made in the reign of Edward III., it was ordained, "that such as were to be admitted Master Masons, or Masters of work, should be examined whether they be able of cunning to serve their respective Lords, as well the lowest as the highest, to the honor and worship of the aforesaid art, and to the profit of their Lords."

Here, then, we may see the origin of that usage, which is still practiced in every well governed lodge, not only of demanding a proper degree of proficiency in the candidate, but also of testing that proficiency by an examination.

This cautious and honest fear of the fraternity, lest any Brother should assume the duties of a position which he could not faithfully discharge, and which is, in our time, tantamount to a candidate's advancing to a degree for which he is not prepared, is again exhibited in the charges enacted in the reign of James II., the manuscript of which was preserved in the archives of the Lodge of Antiquity in London. In these charges it is required, "that no Mason take on no lord's worke, nor any other man's, unless he know himselfe well able to perform the worke, so that the craft have no slander." In the same charges, it is prescribed that "no master, or fellow, shall take no apprentice for less than seven years."

In another series of charges, whose exact date is not ascertained, but whose language and orthography indicate their antiquity, it is said: "Ye shall ordain the wisest to be Master of the work; and neither for love nor lineage, riches nor favor, set one over the work[73] who hath but little knowledge, whereby the Master would be evil served, and ye ashamed."

These charges clearly show the great stress that was placed by our ancient Brethren upon the necessity of skill and proficiency, and they have furnished the precedents upon which are based all the similar regulations that have been subsequently applied to Speculative Masonry.

In the year 1722, the Grand Lodge of England ordered the "Old Charges of the Free and Accepted Masons" to be collected from the ancient records, and, having approved of them, they became a part of the Constitutions of Speculative Freemasonry. In these Charges, it is ordained that "a younger Brother shall be in-

---

73   That is, advance him, from the subordinate position of a serving man or Apprentice, to that of a Fellow Craft or journeyman.

structed in working, to prevent spoiling the materials for want of judgment, and for increasing and continuing of brotherly love."

Subsequently, in 1767, it was declared by the Grand Lodge, that "no lodge shall be permitted to make and raise the same Brother, at one and the same meeting, without a dispensation from the Grand Master, or his Deputy;" and, lest too frequent advantage should be taken of this power of dispensation, to hurry candidates through the degrees, it is added that the dispensation, "*on very particular occasions only*, may be requested."

The Grand Lodge of England afterwards found it necessary to be more explicit on this subject, and the regulation of that body is now contained in the following language:

"No candidate shall be permitted to receive more than one degree on the same day, nor shall a higher degree in Masonry be conferred on any Brother at a less interval than four weeks from his receiving a previous degree, nor until he has passed an examination in open lodge in that degree.[74]"

This seems to be the recognized principle on which the fraternity are, at this day, acting in this country. The rule is, perhaps, sometimes, and in some places, in abeyance. A few lodges, from an impolitic desire to increase their numerical strength, or rapidly to advance men of worldly wealth or influence to high stations in the Order, may infringe it, and neglect to demand of their candidates that suitable proficiency which ought to be, in Masonry, an essential recommendation to promotion; but the great doctrine that each degree should be well studied, and the candidate prove his proficiency in it by an examination, has been uniformly set forth by the Grand Lodge of the United States, whenever they

---

74   This is also the regulation of the Grand Lodge of South Carolina.

have expressed an opinion on the subject.

Thus, for instance, in 1845, the late Bro. A.A. Robertson, Grand Master of New York, gave utterance to the following opinion, in his annual address to the intelligent body over which he presided:

"The practice of examining candidates in the prior degrees, before admission to the higher, in order to ascertain their proficiency, is gaining the favorable notice of Masters of lodges, and cannot be too highly valued, nor too strongly recommended to all lodges in this jurisdiction. It necessarily requires the novitiate to reflect upon the bearing of all that has been so far taught him, and consequently to impress upon his mind the beauty and utility of those sublime truths, which have been illustrated in the course of the ceremonies he has witnessed in his progress in the mystic art. In a word, it will be the means of making competent overseers of the work--and no candidate should be advanced, until he has satisfied the lodge, by such examination, that he has made the necessary proficiency in the lower degrees.[75]"

In 1845, the Grand Lodge of Iowa issued a circular to her subordinates, in which she gave the following admonition:

"To guard against hasty and improper work, she prohibits a candidate from being advanced till he has made satisfactory proficiency in the preceding degrees, by informing himself of the lectures pertaining thereto; and to suffer a candidate to proceed who is ignorant in this essential particular, is calculated in a high degree to injure the institution and retard its usefulness."

---

75 Proceedings of Grand Lodge of New York, for 1845. He excepts, of course, from the operation of the rule, those made by dispensation; but this exception does not affect the strength of the principle.

The Grand Lodge of Illinois has practically declared its adhesion to the ancient regulation; for, in the year 1843, the dispensation of Nauvoo Lodge, one of its subordinates, was revoked principally on the ground that she was guilty "of pushing the candidate through the second and third degrees, before he could possibly be skilled in the preceding degree." And the committee who recommended the revocation, very justly remarked that they were not sure that any length of probation would in all cases insure skill, but they were certain that the ancient landmarks of the Order required that the lodge should know that the candidate is well skilled in one degree before being admitted to another.

The Grand Lodges of Massachusetts and South Carolina have adopted, almost in the precise words, the regulation of the Grand Lodge of England, already cited, which requires an interval of one month to elapse between the conferring of degrees. The Grand Lodge of New Hampshire requires a greater probation for its candidates; its constitution prescribes the following regulation: "All Entered Apprentices must work five months as such, before they can be admitted to the degree of Fellow Craft. All Fellow Crafts must work in a lodge of Fellow Crafts three months, before they can be raised to the sublime degree of Master Mason. Provided, nevertheless, that if any Entered Apprentice, or Fellow Craft, shall make himself thoroughly acquainted with all the information belonging to his degree, he may be advanced at an earlier period, at the discretion of the lodge."

But, perhaps, the most stringent rule upon this subject, is that which exists in the Constitution of the Grand Lodge of Hanover, which is in the following words:

"No Brother can be elected an officer of a lodge until he has been three years a Master Mason. A Fellow Craft must work at least one year in that degree, before he can be admitted to the third degree. An Entered Apprentice must remain at least two years in that degree."

It seems unnecessary to extend these citations. The existence of the regulation, which requires a necessary probation in candidates, until due proficiency is obtained, is universally admitted. The ancient constitutions repeatedly assert it, and it has received the subsequent sanction of innumerable Masonic authorities. But, unfortunately, the practice is not always in accordance with the rule. And, hence, the object of this article is not so much to demonstrate the existence of the law, as to urge upon our readers the necessity of a strict adherence to it. There is no greater injury which can be inflicted on the Masonic Order (the admission of immoral persons excepted), than that of hurrying candidates through the several degrees. Injustice is done to the institution, whose peculiar principles and excellencies are never properly presented--and irreparable injury to the candidate, who, acquiring no fair appreciation of the ceremonies through which he rapidly passes, or of the instructions which he scarcely hears, is filled either with an indifference that never afterwards can be warmed into zeal, or with a disgust that can never be changed into esteem. Masonry is betrayed in such an instance by its friends, and often loses the influence of an intelligent member, who, if he had been properly instructed, might have become one of its warmest and most steadfast advocates.

This subject is so important, that I will not hesitate to add to the influence of these opinions the great sanction of Preston's authority.

"Many persons," says that able philosopher of Masonry, "are deluded by the vague supposition that our mysteries are merely nominal; that the practices established among us are frivolous, and that our ceremonies may be adopted, or waived at pleasure. On this false foundation, we find them hurrying through all the degrees of the Order, without adverting to the propriety of one step they pursue, or possessing a single qualification requisite for advancement. Passing through the usual formalities, they consider themselves entitled to rank as masters of the art, solicit and accept offices, and assume the government of the lodge, equally unacquainted with the rules of the institution they pretend to support, or the nature of the trust they engage to perform. The consequence is obvious; anarchy and confusion ensue, and the substance is lost in the shadow. Hence men eminent for ability, rank, and fortune, are often led to view the honors of Masonry with such indifference, that when their patronage is solicited, they either accept offices with reluctance, or reject them with disdain.[76]"

Let, then, no lodge which values its own usefulness, or the character of our institution, admit any candidate to a higher degree, until he has made suitable proficiency in the preceding one, to be always tested by a strict examination in open lodge. Nor can it do so, without a palpable violation of the laws of Masonry.

Section X.
Of Balloting for Candidates in each Degree.

Although there is no law, in the Ancient Constitutions, which

---

76   Preston, edition of Oliver, p. 12 (U.M.L., vol. iii., p. 10).

in express words requires a ballot for candidates in each degree, yet the whole tenor and spirit of these constitutions seem to indicate that there should be recourse to such a ballot. The constant reference, in the numerous passages which were cited in the preceding Section, to the necessity of an examination into the proficiency of those who sought advancement, would necessarily appear to imply that a vote of the lodge must be taken on the question of this proficiency. Accordingly, modern Grand Lodges have generally, by special enactment, required a ballot to be taken on the application of an Apprentice or Fellow Craft for advancement, and where no such regulation has been explicitly laid down, the almost constant usage of the craft has been in favor of such ballot.

The Ancient Constitutions having been silent on the subject of the letter of the law, local usage or regulations must necessarily supply the specific rule.

Where not otherwise provided by the Constitutions of a Grand Lodge or the bye-laws of a subordinate lodge, analogy would instruct us that the ballot, on the application of Apprentices or Fellow Crafts for advancement, should be governed by the same principles that regulate the ballot on petitions for initiation.

Of course, then, the vote should be unanimous: for I see no reason why a lodge of Fellow Crafts should be less guarded in its admission of Apprentices, than a lodge of Apprentices is in its admission of profanes.

Again, the ballot should take place at a stated meeting, so that every member may have "due and timely notice," and be prepared to exercise his "inherent privilege" of granting or withholding his consent; for it must be remembered that the man who was worthy or supposed to be so, when initiated as an Entered Apprentice, may prove to be unworthy when he applies to pass as a Fellow Graft, and every member should, therefore, have the means and opportunity of passing his judgment on that worthiness or unworthiness.

If the candidate for advancement has been rejected once, he may again apply, if there is no local regulation to the contrary. But, in such a case, due notice should be given to all the members, which is best done by making the application at one regular meeting, and voting for it on the next. This, however, I suppose to be only necessary in the case of a renewed application after a rejection. An Entered Apprentice or a Fellow Craft is entitled after due probation to make his application for advancement; and his first application may be balloted for on the same evening, provided it be a regular meeting of the lodge. The members are supposed to know what work is before them to do, and should be there to do it.

But the case is otherwise whenever a candidate for advancement has been rejected. He has now been set aside by the lodge, and no time is laid down in the regulations or usages of the craft for his making a second application. He may never do so, or he may in three months, in a year, or in five years. The members are, therefore, no more prepared to expect this renewed application at any particular meeting of the lodge, than they are to anticipate any entirely new petition of a profane. If, therefore, the second application is not made at one regular meeting and laid over to the next, the possibility is that the lodge may be taken by surprise, and in the words of the old Regulation, "a turbulent member may be imposed on it."

The inexpediency of any other course may be readily seen, from a suppositions case. We will assume that in a certain lodge, A, who is a Fellow Craft, applies regularly for advancement to the third degree. On this occasion, for good and sufficient reasons, two of the members, B and C, express their dissent by depositing black balls. His application to be raised is consequently rejected, and he remains a Fellow Graft. Two or three meetings of the lodge pass over, and at each, B and C are present; but, at the fourth meeting, circumstances compel their absence, and the friends of A, taking advantage of that occurrence, again propose him for advancement; the ballot is forthwith taken, and he is elected and raised on the same evening. The injustice of this course to B and C, and the evil to the lodge and the whole fraternity, in this imposition of one who is probably an unworthy person, will be apparent to every intelligent and right-minded Mason.

I do not, however, believe that a candidate should be rejected, on his application for advancement, in consequence of objections to his moral worth and character. In such a case, the proper course would be to prefer charges, to try him as an Apprentice or Fellow Craft; and, if found guilty, to suspend, expel, or otherwise appropriately punish him. The applicant as well as the Order is, in such a case, entitled to a fair trial. Want of proficiency, or a mental or physical disqualification acquired since the reception of the preceding degree, is alone a legitimate cause for an estoppal of advancement by the ballot. But this subject will be treated of further in the chapter on the rights of Entered Apprentices.

Section XI.
Of the Number to be Initiated at one Communication.

The fourth General Regulation decrees that "no Lodge shall make more than five new Brothers at one time." This regulation has been universally interpreted (and with great propriety) to mean that not more than five degrees can be conferred at the same communication.

This regulation is, however, subject to dispensation by the Grand Master, or Presiding Grand Officer, in which case the number to be initiated, passed, or raised, will be restricted only by the words of the dispensation.

The following, or fifth General Regulation, says that "no man can be made or admitted a member of a particular lodge, without previous notice, one month before, given to the same lodge."

Now, as a profane cannot be admitted an Entered Apprentice, or in other words, a member of an Entered Apprentices' lodge, unless after one month's notice, so it follows that an Apprentice cannot be admitted a member of a Fellow Crafts' lodge, nor a Fellow Craft of a Masters', without the like probation. For the words of the regulation which apply to one, will equally apply to the others. And hence we derive the law, that a month at least must always intervene between the reception of one degree and the advancement to another. But this rule is also subject to a dispensation.

Section XII.
Of Finishing the Candidates of one Lodge in another.

It is an ancient and universal regulation, that no lodge shall interfere with the work of another by initiating its candidates, or passing or raising its Apprentices and Fellow Crafts. Every lodge is supposed to be competent to manage its own business, and ought to be the best judge of the qualifications of its own members, and hence it would be highly improper in any lodge to confer a degree on a Brother who is not of its household.

This regulation is derived from a provision in the Ancient Charges, which have very properly been supposed to contain the fundamental law of Masonry, and which prescribes the principle of the rule in the following symbolical language:

"None shall discover envy at the prosperity of a Brother, nor supplant him or put him out of his work, if he be capable to finish the same; for no man can finish another's work, so much to the Lord's profit, unless he be thoroughly acquainted with the designs and draughts of him that began it."

There is, however, a case in which one lodge may, by consent, legally finish the work of another. Let us suppose that a candidate has been initiated in a lodge at A----, and, before he receives his second degree, removes to B----, and that being, by the urgency of his business, unable either to postpone his departure from A----, until he has been passed and raised, or to return for the purpose of his receiving his second and third degrees, then it is competent for the lodge at A---- to grant permission to the lodge at B---- to confer them on the candidate.

But how shall this permission be given--by a unanimous vote, or merely by a vote of the majority of the members at A----? Here it seems to me that, so far as regards the lodge at A----, the reasons for unanimity no longer exist. There is here no danger that a "fractious member will be imposed on them," as the candidate, when finished, will become a member of the lodge at B----. The question of consent is simply in the nature of a resolution, and may be determined by the assenting votes of a majority of the members at A---. It is, however, to be understood, that if any Brother believes that the candidate is unworthy, from character, of further advancement, he may suspend the question of consent, by preferring charges against him. If this is not done, and the consent of the lodge is obtained, that the candidate may apply to the lodge at B---, then when his petition is read in that lodge, it must, of course, pass through the usual ordeal of a month's probation, and a unanimous vote; for here the old reasons for unanimity once more prevail.

I know of no ancient written law upon this subject, but it seems to me that the course I have described is the only one that could be suggested by analogy and common sense.

Section XIII.
Of the Initiation of Non-residents.

The subject of this section is naturally divided into two branches:--First, as to the initiation by a lodge of a candidate, who, residing in the same State or Grand Lodge jurisdiction, is still not an inhabitant of the town in which the lodge to which he applies is situated, but resides nearer to some other lodge; and, secondly, as to the initiation of a stranger, whose residence is in another State, or under the jurisdiction of another Grand Lodge.

1. The first of these divisions presents a question which is easily answered. Although I can find no ancient regulation on this subject, still, by the concurrent authority of all Grand Lodges in this country, at least, (for the Grand Lodge of England has no such provision in its Constitution,) every lodge is forbidden to initiate any person whose residence is nearer to any other lodge. If, however, such an initiation should take place, although the lodge would be censurable for its violation of the regulations of its superior, yet there has never been any doubt that the initiation would be good and the candidate so admitted regularly made. The punishment must fall upon the lodge and not upon the newly-made Brother.

2. The second division presents a more embarrassing inquiry, on account of the diversity of opinions which have been entertained on the subject. Can a lodge in one State, or Grand Lodge jurisdiction, initiate the resident of another State, and would such initiation be lawful, and the person so initiated a regular Mason, or, to use the technical language of the Order, a Mason made "in due form," and entitled to all the rights and privileges of the Order?

The question is one of considerable difficulty; it has given occasion to much controversy, and has been warmly discussed within the last few years by several of the Grand Lodges of the United States.

In 1847, the Grand Lodge of Alabama adopted the following regulation, which had been previously enacted by the Grand

Lodge of Tennessee:

"Any person residing within the jurisdiction of this Grand Lodge, who has already, or shall hereafter, travel into any foreign jurisdiction, and there receive the degrees of Masonry, such person shall not be entitled to the rights, benefits, and privileges of Masonry within this jurisdiction, until he shall have been regularly admitted a member of the subordinate lodge under this Grand Lodge, nearest which he at the time resides, in the manner provided by the Constitution of this Grand Lodge for the admission of members."

The rule adopted by the Grand Lodge of Maryland is still more stringent. It declares, "that if any individual, from selfish motives, from distrust of his acceptance, or other causes originating in himself, knowingly and willfully travel into another jurisdiction, and there receive the masonic degrees, he shall be considered and held as a clandestine made Mason."

The Grand Lodge of New York, especially, has opposed these regulations, inflicting a penalty on the initiate, and assigns its reasons for the opposition in the following language:

"Before a man becomes a Mason, he is subject to no law which any Grand Lodge can enact. No Grand Lodge has a right to make a law to compel any citizen, who desires, to be initiated in a particular lodge, or in the town or State of his residence; neither can any Grand Lodge forbid a citizen to go where he pleases to seek acceptance into fellowship with the craft; and where there is no right to compel or to forbid, there can be no right to punish; but it will be observed, that the laws referred to were enacted to punish the citizens of Maryland and Alabama, as Masons and Brethren, for doing something before they were Masons and Brethren, which they had a perfect right to do as citizens and freemen; and it must certainly be regarded as an act of deception and treachery by a young Mason, on returning home, to be told, that he is 'a clandestine Mason,' that he 'ought to be expelled,' or, that he cannot be recognized as a Brother till he 'joins a lodge where his residence is,' because he was initiated in New York, in England, or in France, after having heard all his life of the universality and oneness of the institution.[77]"

It seems to us that the Grand Lodge of New York has taken the proper view of the subject; although we confess that we are not satisfied with the whole course of reasoning by which it has arrived at the conclusion. Whatever we may be inclined to think of the inexpediency of making transient persons (and we certainly do believe that it would be better that the character and qualifications of every candidate should be submitted to the inspection of his neighbors rather than to that of strangers), however much we may condemn the carelessness and facility of a lodge which is thus willing to initiate a stranger, without that due examination of his character, which, of course, in the case of non-residents, can seldom be obtained, we are obliged to admit that such makings are legal--the person thus made cannot be called a clandestine Mason, because he has been made in a legally constituted lodge--and as he is a regular Mason, we know of no principle by which he can be refused admission as a visitor into any lodge to which he applies.

Masonry is universal in its character, and knows no distinction of nation or of religion. Although each state or kingdom has its distinct Grand Lodge, this is simply for purposes of conve-

---

77   Transactions of the G.L. of New York, anno 1848, p. 73.

nience in carrying out the principles of uniformity and subor-
dination, which should prevail throughout the masonic system.
The jurisdiction of these bodies is entirely of a masonic character,
and is exercised only over the members of the Order who have
voluntarily contracted their allegiance. It cannot affect the profane, who are, of course, beyond its pale. It is true, that as soon
as a candidate applies to a lodge for initiation, he begins to come
within the scope of masonic law. He has to submit to a prescribed
formula of application and entrance, long before he becomes a
member of the Order. But as this formula is universal in its operation, affecting candidates who are to receive it and lodges which
are to enforce it in all places, it must have been derived from some
universal authority. The manner, therefore, in which a candidate
is to be admitted, and the preliminary qualifications which are
requisite, are prescribed by the landmarks, the general usage, and
the ancient constitutions of the Order. And as they have directed
the *mode how*, they might also have prescribed the *place where*, a
man should be made a Mason. But they have done no such thing.
We cannot, after the most diligent search, find any constitutional
regulation of the craft, which refers to the initiation of non-residents. The subject has been left untouched; and as the ancient and
universally acknowledged authorities of Masonry have neglected
to legislate on the subject, it is now too late for any modern and
local authority, like that of a Grand Lodge, to do so.

A Grand Lodge may, it is true, forbid--as Missouri, South Carolina, Georgia, and several other Grand Lodges have done--the
initiation of non-residents, within its own jurisdiction, because
this is a local law enacted by a local authority; but it cannot travel
beyond its own territory, and prescribe the same rule to another

Grand Lodge, which may not, in fact, be willing to adopt it.

The conclusions, then, at which we arrive no this subject are these: The ancient constitutions have prescribed no regulation on the subject of the initiation of non-residents; it is, therefore, optional with every Grand Lodge, whether it will or will not suffer such candidates to be made within its own jurisdiction; the making, where it is permitted, is legal, and the candidate so made becomes a regular Mason, and is entitled to the right of visitation.

What, then, is the remedy, where a person of bad character, and having, in the language of the Grand Lodge of Maryland, "a distrust of his acceptance" at home, goes abroad and receives the degrees of Masonry? No one will deny that such a state of things is productive of great evil to the craft. Fortunately, the remedy is simple and easily applied. Let the lodge, into whose jurisdiction he has returned, exercise its power of discipline, and if his character and conduct deserve the punishment, let him be expelled from the Order. If he is unworthy of remaining in the Order, he should be removed from it at once; but if he is worthy of continuing in it, there certainly can be no objection to his making use of his right to visit.

Chapter II.
Of the Rights of Entered Apprentices.

In an inquiry into the rights of Entered Apprentices, we shall not be much assisted by the Ancient Constitutions, which, leaving the subject in the position in which usage had established it, are silent in relation to what is the rule. In all such cases, we must, as I have frequently remarked before, in settling the law, have recourse to analogy, to the general principles of equity, and the dictates of common sense, and, with these three as our guides, we shall find but little difficulty in coming to a right conclusion.

At present, an Entered Apprentice is not considered a member of the Lodge, which privilege is only extended to Master Masons. This was not formerly the case. Then the Master's degree was not as indiscriminately conferred as it is now. A longer probation and greater mental or moral qualifications were required to entitle a candidate to this sublime dignity. None were called Master Masons but such as had presided over their Lodges, and the office of Wardens was filled by Fellow Crafts. Entered Apprentices, as well as Fellow Crafts, were permitted to attend the communications of the Grand Lodge, and express their opinions; and, in 1718, it was enacted that every new regulation, proposed in the Grand Lodge, should be submitted to the consideration of even the youngest Entered Apprentice. Brethren of this degree composed, in fact, at that time, the great body of the craft. But, all these things have, since, by the gradual improvement of our organization, undergone many alterations; and Entered Apprentices seem now, by universal consent, to be restricted to a very few rights. They have the right of sitting in all lodges of their degree, of receiving all the instructions which appertain to it, but not of speaking or voting, and, lastly, of offering themselves as candidates for advancement, without the preparatory necessity of a formal written petition.

These being admitted to be the rights of an Entered Apprentice, few and unimportant as they may be, they are as dear to him as those of a Master Mason are to one who has been advanced to that degree; and he is, and ought to be, as firmly secured in their possession. Therefore, as no Mason can be deprived of his rights and privileges, except after a fair and impartial trial, and the verdict of his peers, it is clear that the Entered Apprentice cannot be divested of these rights without just such a trial and verdict.

But, in the next place, we are to inquire whether the privilege of being passed as a Fellow Craft is to be enumerated among these rights? And, we clearly answer, No. The Entered Apprentice has the right of making the application. Herein he differs from a profane, who has no such right of application until he has qualified himself for making it, by becoming an Entered Apprentice. But, if the application is granted, it is *ex gratia*, or, by the favour of the lodge, which may withhold it, if it pleases. If such were not the case, the lodge would possess no free will on the subject of advancing candidates; and the rule requiring a probation and an examination, before passing, would be useless and absurd--because, the neglect of improvement or the want of competency would be attended with no penalty.

It seems to me, then, that, when an Apprentice applies for his second degree, the lodge may, if it thinks proper, refuse to grant it; and that it may express that refusal by a ballot. No trial is necessary, because no rights of the candidate are affected. He is, by a rejection of his request, left in the same position that he formerly occupied. He is still an Entered Apprentice, in good standing; and the lodge may, at any time it thinks proper, reverse its decision and proceed to pass him.

If, however, he is specifically charged with any offense against the laws of Masonry, it would then be necessary to give him a trial. Witnesses should be heard, both for and against him, and he should be permitted to make his defense. The opinion of the lodge should be taken, as in all other cases of trial, and, according to the verdict, he should be suspended, expelled, or otherwise punished.

The effect of these two methods of proceeding is very different. When, by a ballot, the lodge refuses to advance an Entered Apprentice, there is not, necessarily, any stigma on his moral character. It may be, that the refusal is based on the ground that he has not made sufficient proficiency to entitle him to pass. Consequently, his standing as an Entered Apprentice is not at all affected. His rights remain the same. He may still sit in the lodge when it is opened in his degree; he may still receive instructions in that degree; converse with Masons on masonic subjects which are not beyond his standing; and again apply to the lodge for permission to pass as a Fellow Craft.

But, if he be tried on a specific charge, and be suspended or expelled, his moral character is affected. His masonic rights are forfeited; and he can no longer be considered as an Entered Apprentice in good standing. He will not be permitted to sit in his lodge, to receive masonic instruction, or to converse with Masons on masonic subjects; nor can he again apply for advancement until the suspension or expulsion is removed by the spontaneous action of the lodge.

These two proceedings work differently in another respect. The Grand Lodge will not interfere with a subordinate lodge in compelling it to pass an Entered Apprentice; because every lodge is supposed to be competent to finish, in its own time, and its own way, the work that it has begun. But, as the old regulations,

as well as the general consent of the craft, admit that the Grand
Lodge alone can expel from the rights and privileges of Masonry,
and that an expulsion by a subordinate lodge is inoperative until
it is confirmed by the Grand Lodge, it follows that the expulsion of the Apprentice must be confirmed by that body; and that,
therefore, he has a right to appeal to it for a reversal of the sentence, if it was unjustly pronounced.

Let it not be said that this would be placing an Apprentice on
too great an equality with Master Masons. His rights are dear to
him; he has paid for them. No man would become an Apprentice
unless he expected, in time, to be made a Fellow Craft, and then
a Master. He is, therefore, morally and legally wronged when he
is deprived, without sufficient cause, of the capacity of fulfilling
that expectation. It is the duty of the Grand Lodge to see that
not even the humblest member of the craft shall have his rights
unjustly invaded; and it is therefore bound, as the conservator of
the rights of all, to inquire into the truth, and administer equity.
Whenever, therefore, even an Entered Apprentice complains that
he has met with injustice and oppression, his complaint should be
investigated and justice administered.

The question next occurs--What number of black balls should
prevent an Apprentice from passing to the second degree? I answer, the same number that would reject the application of a profane for initiation into the Order. And why should this not be so?
Are the qualifications which would be required of one applying,
for the first time, for admission to the degree of an Apprentice
more than would subsequently be required of the same person on
his applying for a greater favor and a higher honor--that of being advanced to the second degree? Or do the requisitions, which

exist in the earlier stages of Masonry, become less and less with every step of the aspirant's progress? Viewing the question in this light--and, indeed, I know of no other in which to view it--it seems to me to be perfectly evident that the peculiar constitution and principles of our Order will require unanimity in the election of a profane for initiation, of an Apprentice for a Fellow Craft, and of a Fellow Craft for a Master Mason; and that, while no Entered Apprentice can be expelled from the Order, except by due course of trial, it is competent for the lodge, at any time, on a ballot, to refuse to advance him to the second degree. But, let it be remembered that the lodge which refuses to pass an Apprentice, on account of any objections to his moral character, or doubts of his worthiness, is bound to give him the advantage of a trial, and at once to expel him, if guilty, or, if innocent, to advance him when otherwise qualified.

Chapter III.
Of the Rights of Fellow Crafts.

In ancient times there were undoubtedly many rights attached to the second degree which have now become obsolete or been repealed; for formerly the great body of the fraternity were Fellow Crafts, and according to the old charges, even the Grand Master might be elected from among them. The Master and Wardens of Subordinate Lodges always were. Thus we are told that no Brother can be Grand Master, "unless he has been a Fellow Craft before his election," and in the ancient manner of constituting a lodge, contained in the Book of Constitutions[78], it is said that "the candidates, or the new Master and Wardens, being yet among the Fellow Crafts, the Grand Master shall ask his Deputy if he has examined them," etc. But now that the great body of the Fraternity consists of Master Masons, the prerogatives of Fellow Crafts are circumscribed within limits nearly as narrow as those of Entered Apprentices. While, however, Apprentices are not permitted to speak or vote, in ancient times, and up, indeed, to a very late date. Fellow Crafts were entitled to take a part in any discussion in which the lodge, while open in the first or second degree, might engage, but not to vote. This privilege is expressly stated by Preston, as appertaining to a Fellow Craft, in his charge to a candidate, receiving that degree.

"As a Craftsman, in our private assemblies you may offer your sentiments and opinions on such subjects as are regularly introduced in the Lecture, under the superintendence of an experienced Master, who will guard the landmark against encroachment.[79]"

This privilege is not now, however, granted in this country to Fellow Crafts. All, therefore, that has been said in the preceding chapter, of the rights of Entered Apprentices, will equally apply, *mutatis mutandis*, to the rights of Fellow Crafts.

---

78   Edition of 1723, page 71 (U.M.L., vol. xv., book 1, p. 71).
79   Preston, p. 48 (U.M.L., vol, iii., p. 40).

Chapter IV.
Of the Rights of Master Masons.

When a Mason has reached the third degree, he becomes en-titled to all the rights and privileges of Ancient Craft Masonry. These rights are extensive and complicated; and, like his duties, which are equally as extensive, require a careful examination, thoroughly to comprehend them. Four of them, at least, are of so much importance as to demand a distinct consideration. These are the rights of membership, of visitation, of relief, and of burial. To each I shall devote a separate section.

Section I.
Of the Right of Membership.

The whole spirit and tenor of the General Regulations, as well as the uniform usage of the craft, sustain the doctrine, that when a Mason is initiated in a lodge, he has the right, by sign-ing the bye-laws, to become a member without the necessity of submitting to another ballot. In the Constitutions of the Grand Lodge of New York, this principle is asserted to be one of the an-cient landmarks, and is announced in the following words: "Ini-tiation makes a man a Mason; but he must receive the Master's degree, and sign the bye-laws before he becomes a member of the lodge.[80]" If the doctrine be not exactly a landmark (which I

---

80   Const. New York, 1854, p. 13. The Constitutions of the Grand Lodge of England (p. 64) have a similar provision; but they require the Brother to

confess I am not quite prepared to admit), it comes to us almost clothed with the authority of one, from the sanction of universal and uninterrupted usage.

How long before he loses this right by a non-user, or neglect to avail himself of it, is, I presume, a question to be settled by local authority. A lodge, or a Grand Lodge, may affix the period according to its discretion; but the general custom is, to require a signature of the bye-laws, and a consequent enrollment in the lodge, within three months after receiving the third degree. Should a Mason neglect to avail himself of his privilege, he forfeits it (unless, upon sufficient cause, he is excused by the lodge), and must submit to a ballot.

The reason for such a law is evident. If a Mason does not at once unite himself with the lodge in which he was raised, but permits an extended period of time to elapse, there is no certainty that his character or habits may not have changed, and that he may not have become, since his initiation, unworthy of affiliation. Under the general law, it is, therefore, necessary that he should in such case submit to the usual probation of one month, and an investigation of his qualifications by a committee, as well as a ballot by the members.

But there are other privileges also connected with this right of membership. A profane is required to apply for initiation to the lodge nearest his place of residence, and, if there rejected, can never in future apply to any other lodge. But the rule is different with respect to the application of a Master Mason for membership.

A Master Mason is not restricted in his privilege of applica-

express his wish for membership on the day of his initiation.

tion for membership within any geographical limits. All that is required of him is, that he should be an affiliated Mason; that is, that he should be a contributing member of a lodge, without any reference to its peculiar locality, whether near to or distant from his place of residence. The Old Charges simply prescribe, that every Mason ought to belong to a lodge. A Mason, therefore, strictly complies with this regulation, when he unites himself with any lodge, thus contributing to the support of the institution, and is then entitled to all the privileges of an affiliated Mason.

A rejection of the application of a Master Mason for membership by a lodge does not deprive him of the right of applying to another. A Mason is in "good standing" until deprived of that character by the action of some competent masonic authority; and that action can only be by suspension or expulsion. Rejection does not, therefore, affect the "good standing" of the applicant; for in a rejection there is no legal form of trial, and consequently the rejected Brother remains in the same position after as before his rejection. He possesses the same rights as before, unimpaired and undiminished; and among these rights is that of applying for membership to any lodge that he may select.

If, then, a Mason may be a member of a lodge distant from his place of residence, and, perhaps, even situated in a different jurisdiction, the question then arises whether the lodge within whose precincts he resides, but of which he is not a member, can exercise its discipline over him should he commit any offense requiring masonic punishment. On this subject there is, among masonic writers, a difference of opinion. I, however, agree with Brother Pike, the able Chairman of the Committee of Correspondence of Arkansas, that the lodge can exercise such discipline. I contend that a Mason is amenable for his conduct not only to the lodge of which he may be a member, but also to any one within whose jurisdiction he permanently resides. A lodge is the conservator of the purity and the protector of the integrity of the Order within its precincts. The unworthy conduct of a Mason, living as it were immediately under its government, is calculated most injuriously to affect that purity and integrity. A lodge, therefore, should not be deprived of the power of coercing such unworthy Mason, and, by salutary punishment, of vindicating the character of the institution. Let us suppose, by way of example, that a Mason living in San Francisco, California, but retaining his membership in New York, behaves in such an immoral and indecorous manner as to bring the greatest discredit upon the Order, and to materially injure it in the estimation of the uninitiated community. Will it be, for a moment, contended that a lodge in San Francisco cannot arrest the evil by bringing the unworthy Mason under discipline, and even ejecting him from the fraternity, if severity like that is necessary for the protection of the institution? Or will it be contended that redress can only be sought through the delay and uncertainty of an appeal to his lodge in New York? Even if the words of the ancient laws are silent on this subject, reason and justice would seem to maintain the propriety and expediency of the doctrine that the lodge at San Francisco is amply competent to extend its jurisdiction and exercise its discipline over the culprit.

In respect to the number of votes necessary to admit a Master Mason applying by petition for membership in a lodge, there can be no doubt that he must submit to precisely the same conditions as those prescribed to a profane on his petition for initiation.

There is no room for argument here, for the General Regulations are express on this subject.

"No man can be made or *admitted a member* of a particular lodge," says the fifth regulation, "without previous notice one month before given to the said lodge."

And the sixth regulation adds, that "no man can be entered a Brother in any particular lodge, or *admitted to be a member* thereof, without the unanimous consent of all the members of that lodge then present."

So that it may be considered as settled law, so far as the General Regulations can settle a law of Masonry, that a Master Mason can only be admitted a member of a lodge when applying by petition, after a month's probation, after due inquiry into his character, and after a unanimous ballot in his favor.

But there are other rights of Master Masons consequent upon membership, which remain to be considered. In uniting with a lodge, a Master Mason becomes a participant of all its interests, and is entitled to speak and vote upon all subjects that come before the lodge for investigation. He is also entitled, if duly elected by his fellows, to hold any office in the lodge, except that of Master, for which he must be qualified by previously having occupied the post of a Warden.

A Master has the right in all cases of an appeal from the decision of the Master or of the lodge.

A Master Mason, in good standing, has a right at any time to demand from his lodge a certificate to that effect.

Whatever other rights may appertain to Master Masons will be the subjects of separate sections.

Section II.
Of the Right of Visit.

Every Master Mason, who is an affiliated member of a lodge, has the right to visit any other lodge as often as he may desire to do so. This right is secured to him by the ancient regulations, and is, therefore, irreversible. In the "Ancient Charges at the Constitution of a Lodge," formerly contained in a MS. of the Lodge of Antiquity in London, and whose date is not later than 1688[81],it is directed "that every Mason receive and cherish strange fellows when they come over the country, and set them on work, if they will work as the manner is; that is to say, if the Mason have any mould stone in his place, he shall give him a mould stone, and set him on work; and if he have none, the Mason shall refresh him with money unto the next lodge."

This regulation is explicit. It not only infers the right of visit, but it declares that the strange Brother shall be welcomed, "received, and cherished," and "set on work," that is, permitted to participate in the work of your lodge. Its provisions are equally applicable to Brethren residing in the place where the lodge is situated as to transient Brethren, provided that they are affiliated Masons.

In the year 1819, the law was in England authoritatively settled by a decree of the Grand Lodge. A complaint had been preferred against a lodge in London, for having refused admission to some Brethren who were well known to them, alleging that as the lodge was about to initiate a candidate, no visitor could

---

81   Preston, Oliver's Ed., p. 71, _note_ (U.L.M., vol. iii., p. 60).

be admitted until that ceremony was concluded. It was then declared, "that it is the undoubted right of every Mason who is well
known, or properly vouched, to visit any lodge during the time
it is opened for general masonic business, observing the proper
forms to be attended to on such occasions, and so that the Master
may not be interrupted in the performance of his duty.[82]"

A lodge, when not opened for "general masonic business," but
when engaged in the consideration of matters which interest the
lodge alone, and which it would be inexpedient or indelicate to
make public, may refuse to admit a visitor. Lodges engaged in this
way, in private business, from which visitors are excluded, are
said by the French Masons to be opened "*en famille*."

To entitle him to this right of visit, a Mason must be affili-
ated, that is, he must be a contributing member of some lodge.
This doctrine is thus laid down in the Constitutions of the Grand
Lodge of England:

"A Brother who is not a subscribing member to some lodge,
shall not be permitted to visit any one lodge in the town or place
in which he resides, more than once during his secession from
the craft."

A non-subscribing or unaffiliated Mason is permitted to visit
each lodge once, and once only, because it is supposed that this
visit is made for the purpose of enabling him to make a selection
of the one with which he may prefer permanently to unite. But,
afterwards, he loses this right of visit, to discountenance those
Brethren who wish to continue members of the Order, and to
partake of its pleasures and advantages, without contributing to
its support.

---

82   See Oliver, note in Preston, p. 75 (U.M.L., vol. iii, p. 61).

A Master Mason is not entitled to visit a lodge, unless he previously submits to an examination, or is personally vouched for by a competent Brother present; but this is a subject of so much importance as to claim consideration in a distinct section.

Another regulation is, that a strange Brother shall furnish the lodge he intends to visit with a certificate of his good standing in the lodge from which he last hailed. This regulation has, in late years, given rise to much discussion. Many of the Grand Lodges of this country, and several masonic writers, strenuously contend for its antiquity and necessity, while others as positively assert that it is a modern innovation upon ancient usage.

There can, however, I think, be no doubt of the antiquity of certificates. That the system requiring them was in force nearly two hundred years ago, at least, will be evident from the third of the Regulations made in General Assembly, December 27, 1663, under the Grand Mastership of the Earl of St. Albans[83], and which is in the following words:

"3. That no person hereafter who shall be accepted a Freemason, shall be admitted into any lodge or assembly, until he has brought a certificate of the time and place of his acceptation, from the lodge that accepted him, unto the Master of that limit or division where such a lodge is kept." This regulation has been reiterated on several occasions, by the Grand Lodge of England in 1772, and at subsequent periods by several Grand Lodges of this and other countries. It is not, however, in force in many of the American jurisdictions.

Another right connected with the right of visitation is, that of demanding a sight of the Warrant of Constitution. This instru-

83   Oliver's Preston, p. 162 (U.M.L., vol. iii., p. 135.)

ment it is, indeed, not only the right but the duty of every strange visitor carefully to inspect, before he enters a lodge, that he may thus satisfy himself of the legality and regularity of its character and authority. On such a demand being made by a visitor for a sight of its Warrant, every lodge is bound to comply with the requisition, and produce the instrument. The same rule, of course, applies to lodges under dispensation, whose Warrant of Dispensation supplies the place of a Warrant of Constitution.

Section III.
Of the Examination of Visitors.

It has already been stated, in the preceding section, that a Master Mason is not permitted to visit a lodge unless he previously submits to an examination, or is personally vouched for by some competent Brother present. The prerogative of vouching for a Brother is an important one, and will constitute the subject of the succeeding section. At present let us confine ourselves to the consideration of the mode of examining a visitor.

Every visitor, who offers himself to the appointed committee of the lodge for examination, is expected, as a preliminary step, to submit to the Tiler's Obligation; so called, because it is administered in the Tiler's room. As this obligation forms no part of the secret ritual of the Order, but is administered to every person before any lawful knowledge of his being a Mason has been received, there can be nothing objectionable in inserting it here, and in fact, it will be advantageous to have the precise words of so important a declaration placed beyond the possibility of change or omission by inexperienced Brethren.

The oath, then, which is administered to the visitor, and which he may, if he chooses, require every one present to take with him, is in the following words

"I, A. B., do hereby and hereon solemnly and sincerely swear, that I have been regularly initiated, passed, and raised, to the sublime degree of a Master Mason, in a just and legally constituted lodge of such, that I do not now stand suspended or expelled, and know of no reason why I should not hold masonic communication with my Brethren.

This declaration having been given in the most solemn manner, the examination must then be conducted with the necessary forms. The good old rule of "commencing at the beginning" should be observed. Every question is to be asked and every answer demanded which is necessary to convince the examiner that the party examined is acquainted with what he ought to know, to entitle him to the appellation of a Brother. Nothing is to be taken for granted--categorical answers must be required to all that it is deemed important to be asked. No forgetfulness is to be excused, nor is the want of memory to be accepted as a valid excuse for the want of knowledge. The Mason, who is so unmindful of his duties as to have forgotten the instructions he has received, must pay the penalty of his carelessness, and be deprived of his contemplated visit to that society whose secret modes of recognition he has so little valued as not to have treasured them in his memory. While there are some things which may be safely passed over in the examination of one who confesses himself to be "rusty," or but recently initiated, because they are details which require much study to acquire, and constant practice to retain, there are still other things of great importance which must be rigidly demanded, and with the knowledge of which the examiner cannot, under any circumstances, dispense.

Should suspicions of imposture arise, let no expression of these suspicions be made until the final decree for rejection is pronounced. And let that decree be uttered in general terms, such as: "I am not satisfied," or, "I do not recognize you," and not in more specific terms, such as, "You did not answer this inquiry," or, "You are ignorant on that point." The visitor is only entitled to know, generally, that he has not complied with the requisitions of his examiner. To descend to particulars is always improper and often dangerous.

Above all, the examiner should never ask what are called "leading questions," or such as include in themselves an indication of what the answer is to be; nor should he in any manner aid the memory of the party examined by the slightest hint. If he has it in him, it will come out without assistance, and if he has it not, he is clearly entitled to no aid.

Lastly, never should an unjustifiable delicacy weaken the rigor of these rules. Let it be remembered, that for the wisest and most evident reasons, the merciful maxim of the law, which says, that it is better that ninety-nine guilty men should escape than that one innocent man should be punished, is with us reversed, and that in Masonry *it is better that ninety and nine true men should be turned away from the door of a lodge than that one cowan should be admitted*.

Section IV.
Of Vouching for a Brother.

An examination may sometimes be omitted when any competent Brother present will vouch for the visitor's masonic standing and qualifications. This prerogative of vouching is an important one which every Master Mason is entitled, under certain restrictions, to exercise; but it is also one which may so materially affect the well-being of the whole fraternity--since by its injudicious use impostors might be introduced among the faithful--that it should be controlled by the most stringent regulations.

To vouch for one, is to bear witness for him; and, in witnessing to truth, every caution should be observed, lest falsehood should cunningly assume its garb. The Brother who vouches should, therefore, know to a certainty that the one for whom he vouches is really what he claims to be. He should know this not from a casual conversation, nor a loose and careless inquiry, but, as the unwritten law of the Order expresses it, from "strict trial, due examination, or lawful information."

Of strict trial and due examination I have already treated in the preceding section; and it only remains to say, that when the vouching is founded on the knowledge obtained in this way, it is absolutely necessary that the Brother so vouching shall be *competent* to conduct such an examination, and that his general intelligence and shrewdness and his knowledge of Masonry shall be such as to place him above the probability of being imposed upon. The important and indispensable qualification of a voucher is, therefore, that he shall be competent. The Master of a lodge has no right to accept, without further inquiry, the avouchment of a young and inexperienced, or even of an old, if ignorant, Mason.

Lawful information, which is the remaining ground for an avouchment, may be derived either from the declaration of another Brother, or from having met the party vouched for in a lodge on some previous occasion.

If the information is derived from another Brother, who states that he has examined the party, then all that has already been said of the competency of the one giving the information is equally applicable. The Brother, giving the original information, must be competent to make a rigid examination. Again, the person giving the information, the one receiving it, and the one of whom it is given, should be all present at the time; for otherwise there would be no certainty of identity. Information, therefore, given by letter or through a third party, is highly irregular. The information must also be positive, not founded on belief or opinion, but derived from a legitimate source. And, lastly, it must not have been received casually, but for the very purpose of being used for masonic purposes. For one to say to another in the course of a desultory conversation: "A.B. is a Mason," is not sufficient. He may not be speaking with due caution, under the expectation that his words will be considered of weight. He must say something to this effect: "I know this man to be a Master Mason," for such or such reasons, and you may safely recognize him as such. This alone will insure the necessary care and proper observance of prudence.

If the information given is on the ground that the person, vouched has been seen sitting in a lodge by the voucher, care must be taken to inquire if it was a "Lodge of Master Masons." A person may forget, from the lapse of time, and vouch for a stranger as a Master Mason, when the lodge in which he saw him was only opened in the first or second degree.

Section V.
Of the Right of Claiming Relief.

One of the great objects of our institution is, to afford relief to a worthy, distressed Brother. In his want and destitution, the claim of a Mason upon his Brethren is much greater than that of a profane. This is a Christian as well as a masonic doctrine. "As we have therefore opportunity," says St. Paul, "let us do good unto all men, especially unto them who are of the household of faith."

This claim for relief he may present either to a lodge or to a Brother Mason. The rule, as well as the principles by which it is to be regulated, is laid down in that fundamental law of Masonry, the Old Charges, in the following explicit words, under the head of "Behavior towards a strange Brother:"

"You are cautiously to examine him, in such a method as prudence shall direct you, that you may not be imposed upon by an ignorant, false pretender, whom you are to reject with contempt and derision, and beware of giving him any hints of knowledge.

"But if you discover him to be a true and genuine Brother, you are to respect him accordingly; and if he is in want, you must relieve him if you can, or else direct him how he may be relieved. You must employ him some days, or else recommend him to be employed. But you are not charged to do beyond your ability, only to prefer a poor Brother, that is a good man and true, before any other people in the same circumstances."

This law thus laid down, includes, it will be perceived, as two important prerequisites, on which to found a claim for relief, that the person applying shall be in distress, and that he shall be worthy of assistance.

He must be in distress. Ours is not an insurance company, a joint stock association, in which, for a certain premium paid, an equivalent may be demanded. No Mason, or no lodge, is bound to give pecuniary or other aid to a Brother, unless he really needs. The word " benefit," as usually used in the modern friendly societies, has no place in the vocabulary of Freemasonry. If a wealthy Brother is afflicted with sorrow or sickness, we are to strive to comfort him with our sympathy, our kindness, and our attention, but we are to bestow our eleemosynary aid only on the indigent or the destitute.

He must also be worthy. There is no obligation on a Mason to relieve the distresses, however real they may be, of an unworthy Brother. The claimant must be, in the language of the Charge, "true and genuine." True here is used in its good old Saxon meaning, of "faithful" or "trusty." A true Mason is one who is mindful of his obligations, and who faithfully observes and practices all his duties. Such a man, alone, can rightfully claim the assistance of his Brethren.

But a third provision is made in the fundamental law; namely, that the assistance is not to be beyond the ability of the giver. One of the most important landmarks, contained in our unwritten law, more definitely announces this provision, by the words, that the aid and assistance shall be without injury to oneself or his family. Masonry does not require that we shall sacrifice our own welfare to that of a Brother; but that with prudent liberality, and a just regard to our own worldly means, we shall give of the means with which Providence may have blessed us for the relief of our distressed Brethren.

It is hardly necessary to say, that the claim for relief of a worthy distressed Mason extends also to his immediate family.

Section VI.
Of the Right of Masonic Burial.

After a very careful examination, I can find nothing in the old charges or General Regulations, nor in any other part of the fundamental law, in relation to masonic burial of deceased Brethren. It is probable that, at an early period, when the great body of the craft consisted of Entered Apprentices, the usage permitted the burial of members, of the first or second degree, with the honors of Masonry. As far back as 1754, processions for the purpose of burying Masons seemed to have been conducted by some of the lodges with either too much frequency, or some other irregularity; for, in November of that year, the Grand Lodge adopted a regulation, forbidding them, under a heavy penalty, unless by permission of the Grand Master, or his Deputy[84]. As there were, comparatively speaking, few Master Masons at that period, it seems a natural inference that most of the funeral processions were for the burial of Apprentices, or, at least, of Fellow Crafts.

But the usage since then, has been greatly changed; and by universal consent, the law, as first committed to writing, by Preston, who was the author of our present funeral service, is now

84   See Anderson's Const., 3d Edit., 1755, page 303.

adopted.

The Regulation, as laid down by Preston, is so explicit, that I prefer giving it in his own words[85].

"No Mason can be interred with the formalities of the Order, unless it be at his own special request, communicated to the Master of the Lodge of which he died a member--foreigners and sojourners excepted; nor unless he has been advanced to the third degree of Masonry, from which restriction there can be no exception. Fellow Crafts or Apprentices are not entitled to the funeral obsequies."

This rule has been embodied in the modern Constitutions of the Grand Lodge of England; and, as I have already observed, appears by universal consent to have been adopted as the general usage.

The necessity for a dispensation, which is also required by the modern English Constitutions, does not seem to have met with the same general approval, and in this country, dispensations for funeral processions are not usually, if at all, required. Indeed, Preston himself, in explaining the law, says that it was not intended to restrict the privileges of the regular lodges, but that, "by the universal practice of Masons, every regular lodge is authorized by the Constitution to act on such occasions when limited to its own members.[86]"

It is only when members of other lodges, not under the control of the Master, are convened, that a dispensation is required. But in America, Grand Lodges or Grand Masters have not generally interfered with the rights of the lodges to bury the dead; the

---

85   Preston, Oliver's Edit., p. 89 (U.M.L., vol. iii., p. 72).
86   Preston, Oliver's Edit" p. 90 (U.M.L., vol. iii., p. 73).

Master being of course amenable to the constituted authorities for any indecorum or impropriety.

Chapter V.
Of the Rights of Past Masters.

I have already discussed the right of Past Masters to become members of a Grand Lodge, in a preceding part of this work[87], and have there arrived at the conclusion that no such inherent right exists, and that a Grand Lodge may or may not admit them to membership, according to its own notion of expediency. Still the fact, that they are competent by their masonic rank of accepting such a courtesy when extended, in itself constitutes a prerogative; for none but Masters, Wardens, or Past Masters, can under any circumstances become members of a Grand Lodge.

Past Masters possess a few other positive rights.

In the first place they have a right to install their successors, and at all times subsequent to their installation to be present at the ceremony of installing Masters of lodges. I should scarcely have deemed it necessary to dwell upon so self-evident a proposition, were it not that it involves the discussion of a question which has of late years been warmly mooted in some jurisdictions, namely, whether this right of being present at an installation should, or should not, be extended to Past Masters, made in Royal Arch Chapters.

In view of the fact, that there are two very different kinds of possessors of the same degree, the Grand Lodge of England

87   Book I., chap. iii.

has long since distinguished them as "virtual" and as "actual" Past Masters. The terms are sufficiently explicit, and have the advantage of enabling us to avoid circumlocution, and I shall, therefore, adopt them.

An *actual Past Master* is one who has been regularly installed to preside over a symbolic lodge under the jurisdiction of a Grand Lodge. A *virtual Past Master* is one who has received the degree in a chapter, for the purpose of qualifying him for exaltation to the Royal Arch.

Now the question to be considered is this. Can a virtual Past Master be permitted to be present at the installation of an actual Past Master?

The Committee of Correspondence of New York, in 1851, announced the doctrine, that a Chapter, or virtual Past Master, cannot legally install the Master of a Symbolic Lodge; but that there is no rule forbidding his being present at the ceremony. This doctrine has been accepted by several Grand Lodges, while others again refuse to admit the presence of a virtual Past Master at the installation-service.

In South Carolina, for instance, by uninterrupted usage, virtual Past Masters are excluded from the ceremony of installation.

In Louisiana, under the high authority of the late Brother Gedge, it is asserted, that "it is the bounden duty of all Grand Lodges to prevent the possessors of the (chapter) degree from the exercise of any function appertaining to the office and attributes of an installed Master of a lodge of Symbolic Masonry, and refuse to recognize them as belonging to the order of Past Masters."[88]

Brother Albert Pike, whose opinion on masonic jurispru-

88   Proceedings of Louisiana, an. 1852.

dence is entitled to the most respectful consideration, has announced a similar doctrine in one of his elaborate reports to the Grand Chapter of Arkansas. He does not consider "that the Past Master's degree, conferred in a chapter, invests the recipient with any rank or authority, except within the chapter itself; that it no ways qualifies or authorizes him to preside in the chair of a lodge: that a lodge has no legal means of knowing that he has received the degree in a chapter: for it is not supposed to know anything that takes place there any more than it knows what takes place in a Lodge of Perfection, or a Chapter of Knights of the Rose Croix;" and, of course, if the Past Masters of a lodge have no such "legal means" of recognition of Chapter Masters, they cannot permit them to be present at an installation.

This is, in fact, no new doctrine. Preston, in his description of the installation ceremony, says: "The new Master is then conducted to an adjacent room, where he is regularly installed, and bound to his trust in ancient form, in the presence of at least *three installed Masters*[89]" And Dr. Oliver, in commenting on this passage, says, "this part of the ceremony can only be orally communicated, nor can any but *installed* Masters be present.[90]"

And this rule appears to be founded on the principles of reason. There can be no doubt, if we carefully examine the history of Masonry in this country and in England, that the degree of Past Master was originally conferred by Symbolic Lodges as an honorarium or reward bestowed upon those Brethren who had been found worthy to occupy the Oriental Chair. In so far it was only a degree of office, and could be obtained only from the Lodge

---

89   Preston, Oliver's Edit., p. 76 (U.M.L., vol. iii, p. 62).
90   Ibid

in which the office had been conferred. At a later period it was deemed an essential prerequisite to exaltation in the degree of Royal Arch, and was, for that purpose, conferred on candidates for that position, while the Royal Arch degree was under the control of the symbolic Lodges, but still only conferred by the Past Masters of the Lodge. But subsequently, when the system of Royal Arch Masonry was greatly enlarged and extended in this country, and chapters were organized independent of the Grand and symbolic Lodges, these Chapters took with them the Past Master's degree, and assumed the right of conferring it on their candidates. Hence arose the anomaly which now exists in American Masonry, of two degrees bearing the same name, and said to be almost identical in character, conferred by two different bodies under entirely different qualifications and for totally different purposes. As was to be expected, when time had in some degree obliterated the details of history, each party began to claim for itself the sovereign virtue of legitimacy. The Past Masters of the Chapters denied the right of the Symbolic Lodges to confer the degree, and the latter, in their turn, asserted that the degree, as conferred in the Chapter, was an innovation.

The prevalence of the former doctrine would, of course, tend to deprive the Symbolic Lodges of a vested right held by them from the most ancient times--that, namely, of conferring an honorarium on their Masters elect.

On the whole, then, from this view of the surreptitious character of the Chapter Degree, and supported by the high authority whom I have cited, as well as by the best usage, I am constrained to believe that the true rule is, to deny the Chapter, or Virtual Past Masters, the right to install, or to be present at the installation of the Master of a Symbolic Lodge. A Past Master may preside over a lodge in the absence of the Master, provided he is invited to do so by the Senior Warden present. The Second General Regulation gave the power of presiding, during the absence of the Master, to the last Past Master present, after the lodge had been congregated by the Senior Warden; but two years afterwards, the rule was repealed, and the power of presiding in such cases was vested in the Senior Warden. And accordingly, in this country, it has always been held, that in the absence of the Master, his authority descends to the Senior Warden, who may, however, by courtesy, offer the chair to a Past Master present, after the lodge has been congregated. Some jurisdictions have permitted a Past Master to preside in the absence of the Master and both Wardens, provided he was a member of that lodge. But I confess that I can find no warrant for this rule in any portion of our fundamental laws. The power of congregating the lodge in the absence of the Master has always been confined to the Wardens; and it therefore seems to me, that when both the Master and Wardens are absent, although a Past Master may be present, the lodge cannot be opened.

A Past Master is eligible for election to the chair, without again passing through the office of a Warden.

He is also entitled to a seat in the East, and to wear a jewel and collar peculiar to his dignity.

By an ancient regulation, contained in the Old Charges, Past Masters alone were eligible to the office of Grand Warden. The Deputy Grand Master was also to be selected from among the Masters, or Past Masters of Lodges. No such regulation was in existence as to the office of Grand Master, who might be selected from the mass of the fraternity. At the present time, in this country, it is usual to select the Grand officers from among the Past Masters of the jurisdiction, though I know of no ancient law making such a regulation obligatory, except in respect to the affairs of Grand Wardens and Deputy Grand Master.

Chapter VI.
Of Affiliation.

Affiliation is defined to be the act by which a lodge receives a Mason among its members. A profane is said to be "initiated," but a Mason is "affiliated.[91]"

Now the mode in which a Mason becomes affiliated with a lodge, in some respects differs from, and in others resembles, the mode in which a profane is initiated.

A Mason, desiring to be affiliated with a lodge, must apply by petition; this petition must be referred to a committee for investigation of character, he must remain in a state of probation for one month, and must then submit to a ballot, in which unanimity will be required for his admission. In all these respects, there is no difference in the modes of regulating applications for initiation and affiliation. The Fifth and Sixth General Regulations, upon which these usages are founded, draw no distinction between the act of making a Mason and admitting a member. The two processes are disjunctively connected in the language of both regulations. "No man can be made, *or admitted a member* * * * * without previous notice one month before;" are the words of the Fifth Regulation. And in a similar spirit the Sixth adds: "But no man can be en-

91   See Mackey's Lexicon of Freemasonry, _in voce_.

tered a Brother in any particular lodge, *or admitted to be a member thereof*, without the unanimous consent of all the members of that lodge."

None but Master Masons are permitted to apply for affiliation; and every Brother so applying must bring to the lodge to which he applies a certificate of his regular dismission from the lodge of which he was last a member. This document is now usually styled a "demit," and should specify the good standing of the bearer at the time of his resignation or demission.

Under the regulations of the various Grand Lodges of this country, a profane cannot, as has been already observed, apply for initiation in any other lodge than the one nearest to his residence. No such regulation, however, exists in relation to the application of a Mason for affiliation. Having once been admitted into the Order, he has a right to select the lodge with which he may desire to unite himself. He is not even bound to affiliate with the lodge in which he was initiated, but after being raised, may leave it, without signing the bye-laws, and attach himself to another.

A profane, having been rejected by a lodge, can never apply to any other for initiation. But a Mason, having been rejected, on his application for affiliation, by a lodge, is not thereby debarred from subsequently making a similar application to any other.

In some few jurisdictions a local regulation has of late years been enacted, that no Mason shall belong to more than one lodge. It is, I presume, competent for a Grand Lodge to enact such a regulation; but where such enactment has not taken place, we must be governed by the ancient and general principle.

The General Regulations, adopted in 1721, contain no reference to this case; but in a new regulation, adopted on the 19th February, 1723, it was declared that "no Brother shall belong to more than one lodge within the bills of mortality." This rule was, therefore, confined to the lodges in the city of London, and did not affect the country lodges. Still, restricted as it was in its operation, Anderson remarks, "this regulation is neglected for several reasons, and now obsolete.[92]" Custom now in England and in other parts of Europe, as well as in some few portions of this country, is adverse to the regulation; and where no local law exists in a particular jurisdiction, I know of no principle of masonic jurisprudence which forbids a Mason to affiliate himself with more than one lodge.

The only objection to it is one which must be urged, not by the Order, but by the individual. It is, that his duties and his responsibilities are thus multiplied, as well as his expenses. If he is willing to incur all this additional weight in running his race of Masonry, it is not for others to resist this exuberance of zeal. The Mason, however, who is affiliated with more than one lodge, must remember that he is subject to the independent jurisdiction of each; may for the same offense be tried in each, and, although acquitted by all except one, that, if convicted by that one, his conviction will, if he be suspended or expelled, work his suspension or expulsion in all the others.

---

92   Constitutions, Second Edition of 1738, p. 154.

Chapter VII.
Of Demitting.

To demit from a lodge is to resign one's membership, on which occasion a certificate of good standing and a release from all dues is given to the applicant, which is technically called a *demit*.

The right to demit or resign never has, until within a few years, been denied. In 1853, the Grand Lodge of Connecticut adopted a regulation "that no lodge should grant a demit to any of its members, except for the purpose of joining some other lodge; and that no member shall be considered as having withdrawn from one lodge until he has actually become a member of another." Similar regulations have been either adopted or proposed by a few other Grand Lodges, but I much doubt both their expediency and their legality. This compulsory method of keeping Masons, after they have once been made, seems to me to be as repugnant to the voluntary character of our institution as would be a compulsory mode of making them in the beginning. The expediency of such a regulation is also highly questionable. Every candidate is required to come to our doors "of his own free will and accord," and surely we should desire to keep none among us after that free will is no longer felt. We are all familiar with the Hudibrastic adage, that

"A man convinced against his will,   Is of the same opinion still,"

and he who is no longer actuated by that ardent esteem for the institution which would generate a wish to continue his membership, could scarcely have his slumbering zeal awakened, or his coldness warmed by the bolts and bars of a regulation that should keep him a reluctant prisoner within the walls from which he would gladly escape. Masons with such dispositions we can gladly spare from our ranks.

The Ancient Charges, while they assert that every Mason should belong to a lodge, affix no penalty for disobedience. No man can be compelled to continue his union with a society, whether it be religious, political, or social, any longer than will suit his own inclinations or sense of duty. To interfere with this inalienable prerogative of a freeman would be an infringement on private rights. A Mason's initiation was voluntary, and his continuance in the Order must be equally so.

But no man is entitled to a demit, unless at the time of demanding it he be in good standing and free from all charges. If under charges for crime, he must remain and abide his trial, or if in arrears, must pay up his dues.

There is, however, one case of demission for which a special law has been enacted. That is, when several Brethren at the same time request demits from a lodge. As this action is sometimes the result of pique or anger, and as the withdrawal of several members at once might seriously impair the prosperity, or perhaps even endanger the very existence of the lodge, it has been expressly forbidden by the General Regulations, unless the lodge has become too numerous for convenient working; and not even then is permitted except by a Dispensation. The words of this law are to be found in the Eighth General Regulation, as follows:

"No set or number of Brethren shall withdraw or separate themselves from the lodge in which they were made Brethren, or were afterwards admitted members, unless the lodge becomes too numerous; nor even then, without a dispensation from the Grand Master or his Deputy; and when they are thus separated, they must either immediately join themselves to such other lodge as they shall like best, with the unanimous consent of that other lodge to which they go, or else they must obtain the Grand Master's warrant to join in forming a new lodge."

It seems, therefore, that, although a lodge cannot deny the right of a single member to demit, when a sort of conspiracy may be supposed to be formed, and several Brethren present their petitions for demits at one and the same time, the lodge may not only refuse, but is bound to do so, unless under a dispensation, which dispensation can only be given in the case of an over-populous lodge.

With these restrictions and qualifications, it cannot be doubted that every Master Mason has a right to demit from his lodge at his own pleasure. What will be the result upon himself, in his future relations to the Order, of such demission, will constitute the subject of the succeeding chapter.

Chapter VIII.
Of Unaffiliated Masons.

An unaffiliated Mason is one who is not connected by membership with any lodge. There can be no doubt that such a position is contrary to the spirit of our institution, and that affiliation is a duty obligatory on every Mason. The Old Charges, which have been so often cited as the fundamental law of Masonry, say on this subject: "every Brother ought to belong to a lodge and to be subject to its bye-laws and the General Regulations."

Explicitly as this doctrine has been announced, it has been too little observed, in consequence of no precise penalty having been annexed to its violation. In all times, unaffiliated Masons have existed--Masons who have withdrawn from all active participation in the duties and responsibilities of the Order, and who, when in the hour of danger or distress, have not hesitated to claim its protection or assistance, while they have refused in the day of their prosperity to add anything to its wealth, its power, or its influence. In this country, the anti-masonic persecutions of 1828, and a few years subsequently, by causing the cessation of many lodges, threw a vast number of Brethren out of all direct connection with the institution; on the restoration of peace, and the renewal of labor by the lodges, too many of these Brethren neglected to reunite themselves with the craft, and thus remained unaffiliated. The habit, thus introduced, was followed by others, until the sin of unaffiliation has at length arrived at such a point of excess, as to have become a serious evil, and to have attracted the attention and received the condemnation of almost every Grand Lodge.

A few Grand Lodges have denied the right of a Mason permanently to demit from the Order. Texas, for instance, has declared that "it does not recognize the right of a Mason to demit or separate himself from the lodge in which he was made, or may afterwards be admitted, except for the purpose of joining another lodge, or when he may be about to remove without the jurisdiction of the lodge of which he may be a member.[93]" A few other

93 Proceedings for 1853.

Grand Lodges have adopted a similar regulation; but the prevailing opinion of the authorities appears to be, that it is competent to interfere with the right to demit, certain rights and prerogatives being, however, lost by such demission.

Arkansas, Missouri, Ohio, and one or two other Grand Lodges, while not positively denying the right of demission, have at various times levied a tax or contribution on the demitted or unaffiliated Masons within their respective jurisdictions. This principle, however, has also failed to obtain the general concurrence of other Grand Lodges, and some of them, as Maryland, have openly denounced it. After a careful examination of the authorities, I cannot deny to any man the *right* of withdrawing, whensoever he pleases, from a voluntary association--the laws of the land would not sustain us in the enforcement of such a regulation; and our own self-respect should prevent us from attempting it. If, then, he has a right to withdraw, it clearly follows that we have no right to tax him, which is only one mode of inflicting a fine or penalty for an act, the right to do which we have acceded. In the strong language of the Committee of Correspondence of Maryland[94]: "The object of Masonry never was to extort, nolens volens, money from its votaries. Such are not its principles or teaching. The advocating such doctrines cannot advance the interest or reputation of the institution; but will, as your committee fear, do much to destroy its usefulness. Compulsive membership deprives it of the title, *Free* and Accepted."

But as it is an undoubted precept of the Order that every Mason should belong to a lodge, and contribute, so far as his means will allow, to the support of the institution, and as, by his demis-

94   Proceedings for 1847.

sion, for other than temporary purposes, he violates the principles and disobeys the precepts of the Order, it naturally follows that his withdrawal must place him in a different position from that which he would occupy as an affiliated Mason. It is now time for us to inquire what that new position is.

We may say, then, that, whenever a Mason permanently withdraws his membership, he at once, and while he continues unaffiliated, dissevers all connection between himself and the *Lodge organization* of the Order. He, by this act, divests himself of all the rights and privileges which belong to him as a member of that organization. Among these rights and privileges are those of visitation, of pecuniary aid, and of masonic burial. Whenever he approaches the door of a lodge, asking to enter or seeking for assistance, he is to be met in the light of a profane. He may knock, but the door must not be opened--he may ask, but he is not to receive. The work of the lodge is not to be shared by those who have thrown aside their aprons and their implements, and abandoned the labors of the Temple--the funds of the lodge are to be distributed only among these who are aiding, by their individual contributions, to the formation of similar funds in other lodges.

But from the well-known and universally-admitted maxim of "once a Mason, and always a Mason," it follows that a demitted Brother cannot by such demission divest himself of all his masonic responsibilities to his Brethren, nor be deprived of their correlative responsibility to him. An unaffiliated Mason is still bound by certain obligations, of which he cannot, under any circumstances, divest himself, and by similar obligations are the fraternity bound to him. These relate to the duties of secrecy and of aid in the imminent hour of peril. Of the first of these there can be no doubt; and as to the last, the words of the precept directing it leaves us no option; nor is it a time when the G.H.S. of D. is thrown out to inquire into the condition of the party.

Speaking on this subject, Brother Albert Pike, in his report to the Grand Lodge of Arkansas, says "if a person appeals to us as a Mason in imminent peril, or such pressing need that we have not time to inquire into his worthiness, then, lest we might refuse to relieve and aid a worthy Brother, we must not stop to inquire *as to anything*." But I do not think that the learned Brother has put the case in the strongest light. It is not alone "lest we might refuse to relieve and aid a worthy Brother," that we are in cases of "imminent peril" to make no pause for deliberation. But it is because we are bound by our highest obligations at all times, and to all Masons, to give that aid when *duly* called for.

I may, then, after this somewhat protracted discussion, briefly recapitulate the position, the rights and the responsibilities of an unaffiliated Mason as follows:

1. An unaffiliated Mason is still bound by all his masonic duties and obligations, excepting those connected with the organization of the lodge.

2. He has a right to aid in imminent peril when *he asks for that aid in the proper and conventional way*.

3. He loses the right to receive pecuniary relief.

4. He loses the general right to visit[95] lodges, or to walk in masonic processions.

5. He loses the right of masonic burial.

6. He still remains subject to the government of the Order,

---

95   The right to visit is restricted to once, by many Grand Lodges to enable him to become acquainted with the character of the lodge before he applies for membership.

and may be tried and punished for any offense as an affiliated Mason would be, by the lodge within whose geographical jurisdiction he resides.

Book Fourth.
Of Masonic Crimes and Punishments.

Chapter I.
Of What Are Masonic Crimes.

THE division of wrongs, by the writers on municipal law, into private and public, or civil injuries and crimes and misdemeanors, does not apply to the jurisprudence of Freemasonry. Here all wrongs are crimes, because they are a violation of the precepts of the institution; and an offense against an individual is punished, not so much because it is a breach of his private rights, as because it affects the well-being of the whole masonic community.

In replying to the question, "what are masonic crimes?" by which is meant what crimes are punishable by the constituted authorities, our safest guide will be that fundamental law which is contained in the Old Charges. These give a concise, but succinct summary of the duties of a Mason, and, of course, whatever is a violation of any one of these duties will constitute a masonic crime, and the perpetrator will be amenable to masonic punishment.

But before entering on the consideration of these penal offenses, it will be well that we should relieve the labor of the task, by inquiring what crimes or offenses are not supposed to come within the purview of masonic jurisprudence.

Religion and politics are subjects which it is well known are stringently forbidden to be introduced into Masonry. And hence arises the doctrine, that Masonry will not take congnizance of religious or political offenses.

Heresy, for instance, is not a masonic crime. Masons are obliged to use the words of the Old Charges, "to that religion in which all men agree, leaving their particular opinions to themselves;" and, therefore, as long as a Mason acknowledges his belief in the existence of one God, a lodge can take no action on his peculiar opinions, however heterodox they may be.

In like manner, although all the most ancient and universally-received precepts of the institution inculcate obedience to the civil powers, and strictly forbid any mingling in plots or conspiracies against the peace and welfare of the nation, yet no offense against the state, which is simply political in its character, can be noticed by a lodge. On this important subject, the Old Charges are remarkably explicit. They say, putting perhaps the strongest case by way of exemplifying the principle, "that if a Brother should be a rebel against the State, he is not to be countenanced in his rebellion, however he may be pitied as an unhappy man; and, if convicted of no other crime, though the loyal Brotherhood must and ought to disown his rebellion, and give no umbrage or ground of political jealousy to the government for the time being, they cannot expel him from the lodge, and his relation to it remains indefeasible"

The lodge can, therefore, take no cognizance of religious or political offenses.

The first charge says: "a Mason is obliged by his tenure to obey the moral law." Now, although, in a theological sense, the ten commandments are said to embrace and constitute the moral law, because they are its best exponent, yet jurists have given to the term a more general latitude, in defining the moral laws to be "the eternal, immutable laws of good and evil, to which the Creator himself, in all dispensations, conforms, and which he has enabled human reason to discover, so far as they are necessary for the conduct of human actions.[96]" Perhaps the well known summary of Justinian will give the best idea of what this law is, namely, that we "should live honestly, (that is to say, without reproach,)[97] should injure nobody, and render to every one his just due."

If such, then, be the meaning of the moral law, and if every Mason is by his tenure obliged to obey it, it follows, that all such crimes as profane swearing or great impiety in any form, neglect of social and domestic duties, murder and its concomitant vices of cruelty and hatred, adultery, dishonesty in any shape, perjury or malevolence, and habitual falsehood, inordinate covetousness, and in short, all those ramifications of these leading vices which injuriously affect the relations of man to God, his neighbor, and himself, are proper subjects of lodge jurisdiction. Whatever mor-

96   Blackstone, Introd., Sec. i.
97   For so we should interpret the word "honeste."

al defects constitute the bad man, make also the bad Mason, and consequently come under the category of masonic offenses. The principle is so plain and comprehensible as to need no further exemplification. It is sufficient to say that, whenever an act done by a Mason is contrary to or subsersive of the three great duties which he owes to God, his neighbor, and himself, it becomes at once a subject of masonic investigation, and of masonic punishment.

But besides these offenses against the universal moral law, there are many others arising from the peculiar nature of our institution. Among these we may mention, and in their order, those that are enumerated in the several sections of the Sixth Chapter of the Old Charges. These are, unseemly and irreverent conduct in the lodge, all excesses of every kind, private piques or quarrels brought into the lodge; imprudent conversation in relation to Masonry in the presence of uninitiated strangers; refusal to relieve a worthy distressed Brother, if in your power; and all "wrangling, quarreling, back-biting, and slander."

The lectures in the various degrees, and the Ancient Charges read on the installation of the Master of a lodge, furnish us with other criteria for deciding what are peculiarly masonic offenses. All of them need not be detailed; but among them may be particularly mentioned the following: All improper revelations, undue solicitations for candidates, angry and over-zealous arguments in favor of Masonry with its enemies, every act which tends to impair the unsullied purity of the Order, want of reverence for and obedience to masonic superiors, the expression of a contemptuous opinion of the original rulers and patrons of Masonry, or of the institution itself; all countenance of impostors; and lastly, holding masonic communion with clandestine Masons, or visiting irregular lodges.

From this list, which, extended as it is, might easily have been enlarged, it will be readily seen, that the sphere of masonic penal jurisdiction is by no means limited. It should, therefore, be the object of every Mason, to avoid the censure or reproach of his Brethren, by strictly confining himself as a point within that circle of duty which, at his first initiation, was presented to him as an object worthy of his consideration.

Chapter II.
Of Masonic Punishments.

Having occupied the last chapter in a consideration of what constitute masonic crimes, it is next in order to inquire how these offenses are to be punished; and accordingly I propose in the following sections to treat of the various modes in which masonic law is vindicated, commencing with the slightest mode of punishment, which is censure, and proceeding to the highest, or expulsion from all the rights and privileges of the Order.

Section I.
Of Censure.

A censure is the mildest form of punishment that can be inflicted by a lodge; and as it is simply the expression of an opinion by the members of the lodge, that they do not approve of the conduct of the person implicated, in a particular point of view, and as it does not in any degree affect the masonic standing of the one censured, nor for a moment suspend or abridge his rights and benefits, I have no doubt that it may be done on a mere motion, without previous notice, and adopted, as any other resolution, by a bare majority of the members present.

Masonic courtesy would, however, dictate that notice should be given to the Brother, if absent, that such a motion of censure is about to be proposed or considered, to enable him to show cause, if any he have, why he should not be censured. But such notice is not, as I have said, necessary to the legality of the vote of censure.

A vote of censure will sometimes, however, be the result of a trial, and in that case its adoption must be governed by the rules of masonic trials, which are hereafter to be laid down.

Section II.
Of Reprimand.

A reprimand is the next mildest form of masonic punishment. It should never be adopted on a mere motion, but should always be the result of a regular trial, in which the party may have the opportunity of defense.

A reprimand may be either private or public. If to be given in private, none should be present but the Master and the offender; or, if given by letter, no copy of that letter should be preserved.

If given in public, the lodge is the proper place, and the reprimand should be given by the Master from his appropriate station.

The Master is always the executive officer of the lodge, and in carrying out the sentence he must exercise his own prudent discretion as to the mode of delivery and form of words.

A reprimand, whether private or public, does not affect the masonic standing of the offender.

Section III.
Of Exclusion from the Lodge.

Exclusion from a lodge may be of various degrees.

1. A member may for indecorous or unmasonic conduct be excluded from a single meeting of the lodge. This may be done by the Master, under a provision of the bye-laws giving him the authority, or on his own responsibility, in which case he is amenable to the Grand Lodge for the correctness of his decision. Exclusion in this way does not affect the masonic standing of the person excluded, and does not require a previous trial.

I cannot entertain any doubt that the Master of a lodge has the right to exclude temporarily any member or Mason, when he thinks that either his admission, if outside, or his continuance within, if present, will impair the peace and harmony of the lodge. It is a prerogative necessary to the faithful performance of his duties, and inalienable from his great responsibility to the Grand Lodge for the proper government of the Craft intrusted to his care. If, as it is described in the ancient manner of constituting a lodge, the Master is charged "to preserve the cement of the Lodge," it would be folly to give him such a charge, unless he were invested with the power to exclude an unruly or disorderly member. But as Masters are enjoined not to rule their lodges in an unjust or arbitrary manner, and as every Mason is clearly entitled to redress for any wrong that has been done to him, it follows that the Master is responsible to the Grand Lodge for the manner in which he has executed the vast power intrusted to him, and he may be tried and punished by that body, for excluding a member, when the motives of the act and the other circumstances of the exclusion were not such as to warrant the exercise of his prerogative.

2. A member may be excluded from his lodge for a definite or indefinite period, on account of the non-payment of arrears. This punishment may be inflicted in different modes, and under different names. It is sometimes called, suspension from the lodge, and sometimes *erasure from the roll*. Both of these punishments, though differing in their effect, are pronounced, not after a trial, but by a provision of the bye-laws of the lodge. For this reason alone, if there were no other, I should contend, that they do not affect the standing of the member suspended, or erased, with relation to the craft in general. No Mason can be deprived of his masonic rights, except after a trial, with the opportunity of defense, and a verdict of his peers.

But before coming to a definite conclusion on this subject, it is necessary that we should view the subject in another point of view, in which it will be seen that a suspension from the rights and benefits of Masonry, for the non-payment of dues, is entirely at variance with the true principles of the Order.

The system of payment of lodge-dues does not by any means belong to the ancient usages of the fraternity. It is a modern custom, established for purposes of convenience, and arising out of other modifications, in the organization of the Order. It is not an obligation on the part of a Mason, to the institution at large, but is in reality a special contract, in which the only parties are a particular lodge and its members, of which the fraternity, as a mass, are to know nothing. It is not presented by any general masonic law, nor any universal masonic precept. No Grand Lodge has ever yet attempted to control or regulate it, and it is thus tacitly admitted to form no part of the general regulations of the Order. Even in that Old Charge in which a lodge is described, and the necessity of membership in is enforced, not a word is said of the payment of arrears to it, or of the duty of contributing to its support. Hence the non-payment of arrears is a violation of a special and voluntary contract with a lodge, and not of any general duty to the craft at large. The corollary from all this is, evidently, that the punishment inflicted in such a case should be one affecting the relations of the delinquent with the particular lodge whose bye-laws he has infringed, and not a general one, affecting his relations with the whole Order. After a consideration of all these circumstances, I am constrained to think that suspension from a lodge, for non-payment of arrears, should only suspend the rights of the member as to his own lodge, but should not affect his right of visiting other lodges, nor any of the other privileges inherent in him as a Mason. Such is not, I confess, the general opinion, or usage of the craft in this country, but yet I cannot but believe that it is the doctrine most consonant with the true spirit of the institution. It is the practice pursued by the Grand Lodge of England, from which most of our Grand Lodges derive, directly or indirectly, their existence. It is also the regulation of the Grand Lodge of Massachusetts. The Grand Lodge of South Carolina expressly forbids suspension from the rights and benefits of Masonry for non-payment of dues, and the Grand Lodge of New York has a similar provision in its Constitution.

Of the two modes of exclusion from a lodge for non-payment of dues, namely, suspension and erasure, the effects are very different. Suspension does not abrogate the connection between the member and his lodge, and places his rights in abeyance only. Upon the payment of the debt, he is at once restored without other action of the lodge. But erasure from the roll terminates all connection between the delinquent and the lodge, and he ceases to be a member of it. Payment of the dues, simply, will not restore him; for it is necessary that he should again be elected by the Brethren, upon formal application.

The word exclusion has a meaning in England differing from that in which it has been used in the present section. There the prerogative of expulsion is, as I think very rightly, exercised only by the Grand Lodge. The term "expelled" is therefore used only when a Brother is removed from the craft, by the Grand Lodge. The removal by a District Grand Lodge, or a subordinate lodge, is called "exclusion." The effect, however, of the punishment of exclusion, is similar to that which has been here advocated.

Section IV.
Of Definite Suspension.

Suspension is a punishment by which a party is temporarily deprived of his rights and privileges as a Mason. It does not terminate his connection with the craft, but only places it in abeyance, and it may again be resumed in a mode hereafter to be indicated.

Suspension may be, in relation to time, either definite or in-definite. And as the effects produced upon the delinquent, especially in reference to the manner of his restoration, are different, it is proper that each should be separately considered.

In a case of definite suspension, the time for which the delinquent is to be suspended, whether for one month, for three, or six months, or for a longer or shorter period, is always mentioned in the sentence.

At its termination, the party suspended is at once restored without further action of the lodge. But as this is a point upon which there has been some difference of opinion, the argument will be fully discussed in the chapter on the subject of Restoration.

By a definite suspension, the delinquent is for a time placed beyond the pale of Masonry. He is deprived of all his rights as a Master Mason--is not permitted to visit any lodge, or hold masonic communication with his Brethren--is not entitled to masonic relief, and should he die during his suspension, is not entitled to masonic burial. In short, the amount of punishment differs from that of indefinite suspension or expulsion only in the period of time for which it is inflicted.

The punishment of definite suspension is the lightest that can be inflicted of those which affect the relations of a Mason with the fraternity at large. It must always be preceded by a trial, and the prevalent opinion is, that it may be inflicted by a two-thirds vote of the lodge.

Section V.
Of Indefinite Suspension.

Indefinite suspension is a punishment by which the person suspended is deprived of all his rights and privileges as a Mason, until such time as the lodge which has suspended him shall see fit, by a special action, to restore him.

All that has been said of definite suspension in the preceding section, will equally apply to indefinite suspension, except that in the former case the suspended person is at once restored by the termination of the period for which he was suspended; while in the latter, as no period of termination had been affixed, a special resolution of the lodge will be necessary to effect a restoration.

By suspension the connection of the party with his lodge and with the institution is not severed; he still remains a member of his lodge, although his rights as such are placed in abeyance. In this respect it materially differs from expulsion, and, as an inferior grade of punishment, is inflicted for offenses of a lighter character than those for which expulsion is prescribed.

The question here arises, whether the dues of a suspended member to his lodge continue to accrue during his suspension? I think they do not. Dues or arrears are payments made to a lodge for certain rights and benefits--the exercise and enjoyment of which are guaranteed to the member, in consideration of the dues thus paid. But as by suspension, whether definite or indefinite, he is for the time deprived of these rights and benefits, it would seem unjust to require from him a payment for that which he does not enjoy. I hold, therefore, that suspension from the rights and benefits of Masonry, includes also a suspension from the payment of arrears.

No one can be indefinitely suspended, unless after a due form of trial, and upon the vote of at least two-thirds of the members present.

Section VI.
Of Expulsion.[98]

Expulsion is the very highest penalty that can be inflicted upon a delinquent Mason. It deprives the party expelled of all the masonic rights and privileges that he ever enjoyed, not only as a member of the lodge from which he has been ejected, but also of all those which were inherent in him as a member of the fraternity at large. He is at once as completely divested of his masonic character as though he had never been admitted into the institution. He can no longer demand the aid of his Brethren, nor require from them the performance of any of the duties to which he was formerly entitled, nor visit any lodge, nor unite in any of the public or private ceremonies of the Order. No conversation on masonic subjects can be held with him, and he is to be considered as being completely without the pale of the institution, and to be looked upon in the same light as a profane, in relation to the communication of any masonic information.

It is a custom too generally adopted in this country, for subordinate lodges to inflict this punishment, and hence it is sup-

---

98 I have treated this subject of expulsion so fully in my "Lexicon of Freemasonry," and find so little more to say on the subject, that I have not at all varied from the course of argument, and very little from the phraseology of the article in that work.

posed by many, that the power of inflicting it is vested in the subordinate lodges. But the fact is, that the only proper tribunal to impose this heavy penalty is a Grand Lodge. A subordinate may, indeed, try its delinquent member, and if guilty declare him expelled. But the sentence is of no force until the Grand Lodge, under whose jurisdiction it is working, has confirmed it. And it is optional with the Grand Lodge to do so, or, as is frequently done, to reverse the decision and reinstate the Brother. Some of the lodges in this country claim the right to expel independently of the action of the Grand Lodge, but the claim is not valid. The very fact that an expulsion is a penalty, affecting the general relations of the punished party with the whole fraternity, proves that its exercise never could, with propriety, be intrusted to a body so circumscribed in its authority as a subordinate lodge. Besides, the general practice of the fraternity is against it. The English Constitutions vest the power to expel exclusively in the Grand Lodge[99].

The severity of the punishment will at once indicate the propriety of inflicting it only for the most serious offenses, such, for instance, as immoral conduct, that would subject a candidate for initiation to rejection.

As the punishment is general, affecting the relation of the one expelled with the whole fraternity, it should not be lightly imposed, for the violation of any masonic act not general in its character. The commission of a grossly immoral act is a violation of the contract entered into between each Mason and his Order. If sanctioned by silence or impunity, it would bring discredit on the institution, and tend to impair its usefulness. A Mason

---

99 In England, ejection from a membership by a subordinate lodge is called "exclusion," and it does not deprive the party of his general rights as a member of the fraternity.

who is a bad man, is to the fraternity what a mortified limb is to
the body, and should be treated with the same mode of cure--he
should be cut off, lest his example spread, and disease be propa-
gated through the constitution.

The punishment of expulsion can only be inflicted after a due
course of trial, and upon the votes of at least two-thirds of the
members present, and should always be submitted for approval
and confirmation to the Grand Lodge.

One question here arises, in respect not only to expulsion but
to the other masonic punishments, of which I have treated in the
preceding sections:--Does suspension or expulsion from a Chapter of Royal Arch Masons, an Encampment of Knights Templar,
or any other of what are called the higher degrees of Masonry,
affect the relations of the expelled party to Symbolic or Ancient
Craft Masonry? I answer, unhesitatingly, that it does not, and for
reasons which, years ago, I advanced, in the following language,
and which appear to have met with the approval of the most of
my contemporaries:--

"A chapter of Royal Arch Masons, for instance, is not, and
cannot be, recognized as a masonic body, by a lodge of Master
Masons. 'They hear them so to be, but they do not know them
so to be,' by any of the modes of recognition known to Masonry.
The acts, therefore, of a Chapter cannot be recognized by a Master Masons' lodge, any more than the acts of a literary or chari-
table society wholly unconnected with the Order. Again: By the
present organization of Freemasonry, Grand Lodges are the supreme masonic tribunals. If, therefore, expulsion from a Chapter
of Royal Arch Masons involved expulsion from a Blue Lodge, the
right of the Grand Lodge to hear and determine causes, and to

regulate the internal concerns of the institution, would be interfered with by another body beyond its control. But the converse
of this proposition does not hold good. Expulsion from a Blue
Lodge involves expulsion from all the higher degrees; because,
as they are composed of Blue Masons, the members could not of
right sit and hold communications on masonic subjects with one
who was an expelled Mason.[100]"

Chapter III.
Of Masonic Trials.

Having thus discussed the penalties which are affixed to masonic offenses, we are next to inquire into the process of trial
by which a lodge determines on the guilt or innocence of the
accused. This subject will be the most conveniently considered
by a division into two sections; first, as to the form of trial; and
secondly, as to the character of the evidence.

Section I.
Of the Form of Trial.

Although the authority for submitting masonic offenses to
trials by lodges is derived from the Old Charges, none of the
ancient regulations of the Order have prescribed the details by
which these trials are to be governed. The form of trial must,
therefore, be obtained from the customs and usages of the craft,
and from the regulations which have been adopted by various

100   Lexicon of Freemasonry.

Grand Lodges. The present section will, therefore, furnish a summary of these regulations as they are generally observed in this country.

A charge or statement of the offense imputed to the party is always a preliminary step to every trial.

This charge must be made in writing, signed by the accuser, and delivered to the Secretary, who reads it at the next regular communication of the lodge. A time and place are then appointed by the lodge for the trial.

The accused is entitled to a copy of the charge, and must be informed of the time and place that have been appointed for his trial.

Although it is necessary that the accusation should be preferred at a stated communication, so that no one may be taken at a disadvantage, the trial may take place at a special communication. But ample time and opportunity should always be given to the accused to prepare his defense.

It is not essential that the accuser should be a Mason. A charge of immoral conduct can be preferred by a profane; and if the offense is properly stated, and if it comes within the jurisdiction of the Order or the lodge, it must be investigated. It is not the accuser but the accused that Is to be put on trial, and the lodge is to look only to the nature of the accusation, and not to the individual who prefers it. The motives of the accuser, but not his character, may be examined.

If the accused is living beyond the jurisdiction of the lodge-- that is to say, if he be a member and have removed to some other place without withdrawing his membership, not being a member, or if, after committing the offense, he has left the jurisdiction, the charge must be transmitted to his present place of residence, by mail or otherwise, and a reasonable time be allowed for his answer before the lodge proceeds to trial.

The lodge should be opened in the highest degree to which the accused has attained; and the examinations should take place in the presence of the accused and the accuser (if the latter be a Mason); but the final decision should always be made in the third degree.

The accused and the accuser have a right to be present at all examinations of witnesses, whether those examinations are taken in open lodge or in a committee, and to propose such relevant questions as they desire.

When the trial is concluded, the accused and accuser should retire, and the Master or presiding officer must then put the question of guilty or not guilty to the lodge. Of course, if there are several charges or specifications, the question must be taken on each separately. For the purposes of security and independence in the expression of opinion, it seems generally conceded, that this question should be decided by ballot; and the usage has also obtained, of requiring two-thirds of the votes given to be black, to secure a conviction. A white ball, of course, is equivalent to acquittal, and a black one to conviction.

Every member present is bound to vote, unless excused by unanimous consent.

If, on a scrutiny, it is found that the verdict is guilty, the Master or presiding officer must then put the question as to the amount and nature of the punishment to be inflicted.

He will commence with the highest penalty, or expulsion, and, if necessary, by that punishment being negatived, proceed to propose indefinite and then definite suspension, exclusion, public or private reprimand, and censure.

For expulsion or either kind of suspension, two-thirds of the votes present are necessary. For either of the other and lighter penalties, a bare majority will be sufficient.

The votes on the nature of the punishment should be taken by a show of hands.

If the residence of the accused is not known, or if, upon due summons, he refuses or neglects to attend, the lodge may, nevertheless, proceed to trial without his presence.

In trials conducted by Grand Lodges, it is usual to take the preliminary testimony in a committee; but the final decision must always be made in the Grand Lodge.

Section II.
Of the Evidence in Masonic Trials.

In the consideration of the nature of the evidence that is to be given in masonic trials, it is proper that we should first inquire what classes of persons are to be deemed incompetent as witnesses.

The law of the land, which, in this instance, is the same as the law of Masonry, has declared the following classes of person to be incompetent to give evidence.

1. Persons who have not the use of reason, are, from the infirmity of their nature, considered to be utterly incapable of giving evidence[101]. This class includes idiots, madmen, and children too young to be sensible of the obligations of an oath, and to distin-

101   Phillips, on Evidence, p. 3.

guish between good and evil.

2. Persons who are entirely devoid of any such religious principle or belief as would bind their consciences to speak the truth, are incompetent as witnesses. Hence, the testimony of an atheist must be rejected; because, as it has been well said, such a person cannot be subject to that sanction which is deemed an indispensable test of truth. But as Masonry does not demand of its candidates any other religious declaration than that of a belief in God, it cannot require of the witnesses in its trials any profession of a more explicit faith. But even here it seems to concur with the law of the land; for it has been decided by Chief Baron Willes, that "an infidel who believes in a God, and that He will reward and punish him in this world, but does not believe in a future state, may be examined upon oath."

3. Persons who have been rendered infamous by their conviction of great crimes, are deemed incompetent to give evidence. This rule has been adopted, because the commission of an infamous crime implies, as Sir William Scott has observed, "such a dereliction of moral principle on the part of the witness, as carries with it the conclusion that he would entirely disregard the obligation of an oath." Of such a witness it has been said, by another eminent judge[102], that "the credit of his oath is over-balanced by the stain of his iniquity."

4. Persons interested in the result of the trial are considered incompetent to give evidence. From the nature of human actions and passions, and from the fact that all persons, even the most virtuous, are unconsciously swayed by motives of interest, the testimony of such persons is rather to be distrusted than believed.

102   Chief Baron Gilbert.

This rule will, perhaps, be generally of difficult application in masonic trials, although in a civil suit at law it is easy to define what
is the interest of a party sufficient to render his evidence incompetent. But whenever it is clearly apparent that the interests of
a witness would be greatly benefited by either the acquittal or
the conviction of the accused, his testimony must be entirely rejected, or, if admitted, its value must be weighed with the most
scrupulous caution.

Such are the rules that the wisdom of successive generations
of men, learned in the law, have adopted for the establishment of
the competency or incompetency of witnesses. There is nothing
in them which conflicts with the principles of justice, or with the
Constitutions of Freemasonry; and hence they may, very properly, be considered as a part of our own code. In determining,
therefore, the rule for the admission of witnesses in masonic trials, we are to be governed by the simple proposition that has been
enunciated by Mr. Justice Lawrence in the following language:

"I find no rule less comprehensive than this, that all persons
are admissible witnesses who have the use of their reason, and
such religious belief as to feel the obligation of an oath, who have
not been convicted of any infamous crime, and who are not influenced by interest."

The peculiar, isolated character of our institution, here suggests as an important question, whether it is admissible to take
the testimony of a profane, or person who is not a Freemason, in
the trial of a Mason before his lodge.

To this question I feel compelled to reply, that such testimony
is generally admissible; but, as there are special cases in which it
is not, it seems proper to qualify that reply by a brief inquiry into

the grounds and reasons of this admissibility, and the mode and manner in which such testimony is to be taken.

The great object of every trial, in Masonry, as elsewhere, is to elicit truth; and, in the spirit of truth, to administer justice. From whatever source, therefore, this truth can be obtained, it is not only competent there to seek it, but it is obligatory on us so to do. This is the principle of law as well as of common sense. Mr. Phillips, in the beginning of his great "Treatise on the Law of Evidence," says: "In inquiries upon this subject, the great end and object ought always to be, the ascertaining of the most convenient and surest means for the attainment of truth; the rules laid down are the means used for the attainment of that end."

Now, if A, who is a Freemason, shall have committed an offense, of which B and C alone were cognizant as witnesses, shall it be said that A must be acquitted for want of proof, because B and C are not members of the Order? We apprehend that in this instance the ends of justice would be defeated, rather than subserved. If the veracity and honesty of B and C are unimpeached, their testimony as to the fact cannot lawfully be rejected on any ground, except that they may be interested in the result of the trial, and might be benefited by the conviction or the acquittal of the defendant. But this is an objection that would hold against the evidence of a Mason, as well as a profane.

Any other rule would be often attended with injurious consequences to our institution. We may readily suppose a case by way of illustration. A, who is a member of a lodge, is accused of habitual intemperance, a vice eminently unmasonic in its character, and one which will always reflect a great portion of the degradation of the offender upon the society which shall sustain and defend him in its perpetration. But it may happen--and this is a very conceivable case--that in consequence of the remoteness of his dwelling, or from some other supposable cause, his Brethren have no opportunity of seeing him, except at distant intervals. There is, therefore, no Mason, to testify to the truth of the charge, while his neighbors and associates, who are daily and hourly in his company, are all aware of his habit of intoxication.

If, then, a dozen or more men, all of reputation and veracity, should come, or be brought before the lodge, ready and willing to testify to this fact, by what process of reason or justice, or under what maxim of masonic jurisprudence, could their testimony be rejected, simply because they were not Masons? And if rejected-- if the accused with this weight of evidence against him, with this infamy clearly and satisfactorily proved by these reputable witnesses, were to be acquitted, and sent forth purged of the charge, upon a mere technical ground, and thus triumphantly be sustained in the continuation of his vice, and that in the face of the very community which was cognizant of his degradation of life and manners, who could estimate the disastrous consequences to the lodge and the Order which should thus support and uphold him in his guilty course? The world would not, and could not appreciate the causes that led to the rejection of such clear and unimpeachable testimony, and it would visit with its just reprobation the institution which could thus extend its fraternal affections to the support of undoubted guilt.

But, moreover, this is not a question of mere theory; the principle of accepting the testimony of non-masonic witnesses has been repeatedly acted on. If a Mason has been tried by the courts of his country on an indictment for larceny, or any other infamous crime, and been convicted by the verdict of a jury, although neither the judge nor the jury, nor the witnesses were Masons, no lodge after such conviction would permit him to retain his membership, but, on the contrary, it would promptly and indignantly expel him from the Brotherhood. If, however, the lodge should refuse to expel him, on the ground that his conviction before the court was based on the testimony of non-masonic witnesses, and should grant him a lodge trial for the same offense, then, on the principle against which we are contending, the evidence of these witnesses as "profanes" would be rejected, and the party be acquitted for want of proof; and thus the anomalous and disgraceful spectacle would present itself--of a felon condemned and punished by the laws of his country for an infamous crime, acquitted and sustained by a lodge of Freemasons.

But we will be impressed with the inexpediency and injustice of this principle, when we look at its operation from another point of view. It is said to be a bad rule that will not work both ways; and, therefore, if the testimony of non-masonic witnesses against the accused is rejected on the ground of inadmissibility, it must also be rejected when given in his favor. Now, if we suppose a case, in which a Mason was accused before his lodge of having committed an offense, at a certain time and place, and, by the testimony of one or two disinterested persons, he could establish what the law calls an *alibi*, that is, that at that very time he was at a far-distant place, and could not, therefore, have committed the offense charged against him, we ask with what show of justice or reason could such testimony be rejected, simply because the parties giving it were not Masons? But if the evidence of a "profane" is admitted in favor of the accused, rebutting testimony of the same kind cannot with consistency be rejected; and hence the rule is determined that in the trial of Masons, it is competent to receive the evidence of persons who are not Masons, but whose competency, in other respects, is not denied.

It must, however, be noted, that the testimony of persons who are not Masons is not to be given as that of Masons is, within the precincts of the lodge. They are not to be present at the trial; and whatever testimony they have to adduce, must be taken by a committee, to be afterwards accurately reported to the lodge. But in all cases, the accused has a right to be present, and to interrogate the witnesses.

The only remaining topic to be discussed is the method of taking the testimony, and this can be easily disposed of.

The testimony of Masons is to be taken either in lodge or in committee, and under the sanction of their obligations.

The testimony of profanes is always to be taken by a committee, and on oath administered by a competent legal officer--the most convenient way of taking such testimony is by affidavit.

Chapter IV.
Of the Penal Jurisdiction of a Lodge.

The penal jurisdiction of a lodge is that jurisdiction which it is authorized to exercise for the trial of masonic offenses, and the infliction of masonic punishment. It may be considered as either geographical or personal.

The geographical jurisdiction of a lodge extends in every direction, half way to the nearest lodge. Thus, if two lodges be situated at the distance of sixteen miles from each other, then the penal jurisdiction of each will extend for the space of eight miles in the direction of the other.

The personal jurisdiction of a lodge is that jurisdiction which a lodge may exercise over certain individuals, respective or irrespective of geographical jurisdiction. This jurisdiction is more complicated than the other, and requires a more detailed enumeration of the classes over whom it is to be exercised.

1. A lodge exercises penal jurisdiction over all its members, no matter where they may reside. A removal from the geographical jurisdiction will not, in this case, release the individual from personal jurisdiction. The allegiance of a member to his lodge is indefeasible.

2. A lodge exercises penal jurisdiction over all unaffiliated Masons, living within its geographical jurisdiction. An unaffiliated Mason cannot release himself from his responsibilities to the Order. And if, by immoral or disgraceful conduct, he violates the regulations of the Order, or tends to injure its reputation in the estimation of the community, he is amenable to the lodge nearest to his place of residence, whether this residence be temporary or permanent, and may be reprimanded, suspended, or expelled.

This doctrine is founded on the wholesome reason, that as a lodge is the guardian of the purity and safety of the institution, within its own jurisdiction, it must, to exercise this guardianship with success, be invested with the power of correcting every evil that occurs within its precincts. And if unaffiliated Masons were exempted from this control, the institution might be seriously affected in the eyes of the community, by their bad conduct.

3. The personal jurisdiction of a lodge, for the same good reason, extends over all Masons living in its vicinity. A Master Mason belonging to a distant lodge, but residing within the geographical jurisdiction of another lodge, becomes amenable for his conduct to the latter, as well as to the former lodge. But if his own lodge is within a reasonable distance, courtesy requires that the lodge near which he resides should rather make a complaint to his lodge than itself institute proceedings against him. But the reputation of the Order must not be permitted to be endangered, and a case might occur, in which it would be inexpedient to extend this courtesy, and where the lodge would feel compelled to proceed to the trial and punishment of the offender, without appealing to his lodge. The geographical jurisdiction will, in all cases, legalize the proceedings.

4. But a lodge situated near the confines of a State cannot extend its jurisdiction over Masons residing in a neighboring State, and not being its members, however near they may reside to it: for no lodge can exercise jurisdiction over the members of another Grand Lodge jurisdiction. Its geographical, as well as personal jurisdiction, can extend no further than that of its own Grand Lodge.

5. Lastly, no lodge can exercise penal jurisdiction over its own Master, for he is alone responsible for his conduct to the Grand Lodge. But it may act as his accuser before that body, and impeach him for any offense that he may have committed. Neither can a lodge exercise penal jurisdiction over the Grand Master, although under other circumstances it might have both geographical and personal jurisdiction over him, from his residence and membership.

Chapter V.
Of Appeals.

Every Mason, who has been tried and convicted by a lodge, has an inalienable right to appeal from that conviction, and from the sentence accompanying it, to the Grand Lodge.

As an appeal always supposes the necessity of a review of the whole case, the lodge is bound to furnish the Grand Lodge with an attested copy of its proceedings on the trial, and such other testimony in its possession as the appellant may deem necessary for his defense.

The Grand Lodge may, upon investigation, confirm the verdict of its subordinate. In this case, the appeal is dismissed, and the sentence goes into immediate operation without any further proceedings on the part of the lodge.

The Grand Lodge may, however, only approve in part, and may reduce the penalty inflicted, as for instance, from expulsion to suspension. In this case, the original sentence of the lodge becomes void, and the milder sentence of the Grand Lodge is to be put in force. The same process would take place, were the Grand Lodge to increase instead of diminishing the amount of punishment, as from suspension to expulsion. For it is competent for the Grand Lodge, on an appeal, to augment, reduce or wholly abrogate the penalty inflicted by its subordinate.

But the Grand Lodge may take no direct action on the penalty inflicted, but may simply refer the case back to the subordinate for a new trial. In this case, the proceedings on the trial will be commenced *de novo*, if the reference has been made on the ground of any informality or illegality in the previous trial. But if the case is referred back, not for a new trial, but for further consideration, on the ground that the punishment was inadequate--either too severe, or not sufficiently so--in this case, it is not necessary to repeat the trial. The discussion on the nature of the penalty to be inflicted should, however, be reviewed, and any new evidence calculated to throw light on the nature of the punishment which is most appropriate, may be received.

Lastly, the Grand Lodge may entirely reverse the decision of its subordinate, and decree a restoration of the appellant to all his rights and privileges, on the ground of his innocence of the charges which had been preferred against him. But, as this action is often highly important in its results, and places the appellant and the lodge in an entirely different relative position, I have deemed its consideration worthy of a distinct chapter.

During the pendency of an appeal, the sentence of the subordinate lodge is held in abeyance, and cannot; be enforced. The appellant in this case remains in the position of a Mason "under charges."

Chapter VI.
Of Restoration.

The penalties of suspension and expulsion are terminated by restoration, which may take place either by the action of the lodge which inflicted them, or by that of the Grand Lodge.

Restoration from definite suspension is terminated without any special action of the lodge, but simply by the termination of the period for which the party was suspended. He then at once reenters into the possession of all the rights, benefits, and functions, from which he had been temporarily suspended.

I have myself no doubt of the correctness of this principle; but, as it has been denied by some writers, although a very large majority of the authorities are in its favor, it may be well, briefly, to discuss its merits.

Let us suppose that on the 1st of January A.B. had been suspended for three months, that is, until the 1st day of April. At the end of the three months, that is to say, on the first of April, A.B. would no longer be a suspended member--for the punishment decreed will have been endured; and as the sentence of the lodge had expressly declared that his suspension was to last until the 1st of April, the said sentence, if it means anything, must mean that the suspension was, on the said 1st of April, to cease and determine. If he were, therefore, to wait until the 1st of May for the action of the lodge, declaring his restoration, he would suffer a punishment of four months' suspension, which was not decreed by his lodge upon his trial, and which would, therefore, be manifestly unjust and illegal.

Again: if the offense which he had committed was, upon his trial, found to be so slight as to demand only a dismissal for one night from the lodge, will it be contended that, on his leaving the lodge-room pursuant to his sentence, he leaves not to return to it on the succeeding communication, unless a vote should permit him? Certainly not. His punishment of dismissal for one night had been executed; and on the succeeding night he reentered into the possession of all his rights. But if he can do so after a dismissal or suspension of one night, why not after one or three, six or twelve months? The time is extended, but the principle remains the same.

But the doctrine, that after the expiration of the term of a definite suspension, an action by the lodge is still necessary to a complete restoration, is capable of producing much mischief and oppression. For, if the lodge not only has a right, but is under the necessity of taking up the case anew, and deciding whether the person who had been suspended for three months, and whose period of suspension has expired, shall now be restored, it follows, that the members of the lodge, in the course of their inquiry, are permitted to come to such conclusion as they may think just and fit; for to say that they, after all their deliberations, are, to vote only in one way, would be too absurd to require any consideration. They may, therefore, decide that A.B., having undergone the sentence of the lodge, shall be restored, and then of course all would be well, and no more is to be said. But suppose that they decide otherwise, and say that A.B., having undergone the sentence of suspension of three months, *shall not* be restored, but must remain suspended until further orders. Here, then, a party would have been punished a second time for the same offense, and that, too, after having suffered what, at the time of his conviction, was supposed to be a competent punishment--and without a trial, and without the necessary opportunities of defense, again found guilty, and his comparatively light punishment of suspension for three months changed into a severer one, and of an indefinite period. The annals of the most arbitrary government in the world-- the history of the most despotic tyrant that ever lived--could not

show an instance of more unprincipled violation of law and justice than this. And yet it may naturally be the result of the doctrine, that in a sentence of definite suspension, the party can be
restored only by a vote of the lodge at the expiration of his term
of suspension. If the lodge can restore him, it can as well refuse to
restore him, and to refuse to restore him would be to inflict a new
punishment upon him for an old and atoned-for offense.

On the 1st of January, for instance, A.B., having been put
upon his trial, witnesses having been examined, his defense having been heard, was found guilty by his lodge of some offense,
the enormity of which, whatever it might be, seemed to require
a suspension from Masonry for just three months, neither more
nor less. If the lodge had thought the crime still greater, it would,
of course, we presume, have decreed a suspension of six, nine,
or twelve months. But considering, after a fair, impartial, and
competent investigation of the merits of the case (for all this is
to be presumed), that the offended law would be satisfied with
a suspension of three months, that punishment is decreed. The
court is adjourned *sine die*; for it has done all that is required--
the prisoner undergoes his sentence with becoming contrition,
and the time having expired, the bond having been paid, and the
debt satisfied, he is told that he must again undergo the ordeal of
another trial, before another court, before he can reassume what
was only taken from him for a definite period; and that it is still
doubtful, whether the sentence of the former court may not even
now, after its accomplishment, be reversed, and a new and more
severe one be inflicted.

The analogy of a person who has been sentenced to imprisonment for a certain period, and who, on the expiration of that peri-

od, is at once released, has been referred to, as apposite to the case of a definite suspension. Still more appropriately may we refer to the case of a person transported for a term of years, and who cannot return until that term expires, but who is at liberty at once to do so when it has expired. "Another capital offense against public justice," says Blackstone, "is the returning from transportation, or being seen at large in Great Britain before the expiration of the term for which the offender was sentenced to be transported." Mark these qualifying words: "before the expiration of the term:" they include, from the very force of language, the proposition that it is no offense to return *after* the expiration of the term. And so changing certain words to meet the change of circumstances, but leaving the principle unchanged, we may lay down the law in relation to restorations from definite suspensions, as follows:

It is an offense against the masonic code to claim the privileges of Masonry, or to attempt to visit a lodge after having been suspended, before the expiration of the term for which the offender was suspended.

Of course, it is no crime to resume these privileges after the term has expired; for surely he must have strange notions of the powers of language, who supposes that suspension for three months, and no more, does not mean, that when the three months are over the suspension ceases. And, if the suspension ceases, the person is no longer suspended; and, if no longer suspended he is in good standing, and requires no further action to restore him to good moral and masonic health.

But it is said that, although originally only suspended for three months, at the expiration of that period, his conduct might continue to be such as to render his restoration a cause of public reproach. What is to be done in such a case? It seems strange that the question should be asked. The remedy is only too apparent. Let new charges be preferred, and let a new trial take place for his derelictions of duty during the term of his suspension. Then, the lodge may again suspend him for a still longer period, or altogether expel him, if it finds him deserving such punishment. But in the name of justice, law, and common sense, do not insiduously and unmanfully continue a sentence for one and a former offense, as a punishment for another and a later one, and that, too, without the due forms of trial.

Let us, in this case, go again for an analogy to the laws of the land. Suppose an offender had been sentenced to an imprisonment of six months for a larceny, and that while in prison he had committed some new crime. When the six months of his sentence had expired, would the Sheriff feel justified, or even the Judge who had sentenced him, in saying: "I will not release you; you have guilty of another offense during your incarceration, and therefore, I shall keep you confined six months longer?" Certainly not. The Sheriff or the Judge who should do so high-handed a measure, would soon find himself made responsible for the violation of private rights. But the course to be pursued would be, to arrest him for the new offense, give him a fair trial, and, if convicted again, imprison or otherwise punish him, according to his new sentence, or, if acquitted, discharge him.

The same course should be pursued with a Mason whose conduct during the period of his suspension has been liable to reproach or suspicion. Masons have rights as well as citizens--every one is to be considered innocent until he is proved guilty--and no one should suffer punishment, even of the lightest kind, except after an impartial trial by his peers.

But the case of an indefinite suspension is different. Here no particular time has been appointed for the termination of the punishment. It may be continued during life, unless the court which has pronounced it think proper to give a determinate period to what was before indeterminate, and to declare that on such a day the suspension shall cease, and the offender be restored. In a case of this kind, action on the part of the lodge is necessary to effect a restoration.

Such a sentence being intended to last indefinitely--that is to say, during the pleasure of the lodge--may, I conceive, be reversed at any legal time, and the individual restored by a mere majority vote the of lodge. Some authorities think a vote of two-thirds necessary; but I see no reason why a lodge may not, in this as in other cases, reverse its decision by a vote of a simple majority. The Ancient Constitutions are completely silent on this and all its kindred points; and, therefore, where a Grand Lodge has made no local regulation on the subject, we must be guided by the principles of reason and analogy, both of which direct us to the conclusion that a lodge may express its will, in matters unregulated by the Constitutions, through the vote of a majority.

But the restoration of an expelled Mason requires a different action. By expulsion, as I have already said, all connection with the Order is completely severed. The individual expelled ceases to be a Mason, so far as respects the exercise of any masonic rights or privileges. His restoration to the Order is, therefore, equivalent to the admission of a profane. Having ceased on his expulsion to be a member of the lodge which had expelled him, his restoration would be the admission of a new member. The expelled Mason and the uninitiated candidate are to be placed on the same footing--both are equally unconnected with the institution--the one having never been in it, and the other having been completely discharged from it.

The rule for the admission of new members, as laid down in the Thirty-nine Regulations, seems to me, therefore, to be applicable in this case; and hence, I conceive that to reverse a sentence of expulsion and to restore an expelled Mason will require as unanimous a vote as that which is necessary on a ballot for initiation.

Every action taken by a lodge for restoration must be done at a stated communication and after due notice, that if any member should have good and sufficient reasons to urge against the restoration, he may have an opportunity to present them.

In conclusion, the Grand Lodge may restore a suspended or expelled Mason, contrary to the wishes of the lodge.

In such case, if the party has been suspended only, he, at once, resumes his place and functions in the lodge, from which, indeed, he had only been temporarily dissevered.

But in the case of the restoration of an expelled Mason to the rights and privileges of Masonry, by a Grand Lodge, does such restoration restore him to membership in his lodge? This question is an important one, and has very generally been decided in the negative by the Grand Lodges of this country. But as I unfortunately differ from these high authorities, I cannot refrain, as an apology for this difference of opinion, from presenting the considerations which have led me to the conclusion which I have adopted. I cannot, it is true, in the face of the mass of opposing authority, offer this conclusion as masonic law. But I would fain hope that the time is not far distant when it will become so, by the change on the part of Grand Lodges of the contrary decisions which they have made.

The general opinion in this country is, that when a Mason has been expelled by his lodge, the Grand Lodge may restore him to the rights and privileges, but cannot restore him to membership in his lodge. My own opinion, in contradiction to this, is, that when a Grand Lodge restores an expelled Mason, on the ground that the punishment of expulsion from the rights and privileges of Masonry was too severe and disproportioned to the offense, it may or may not restore him to membership in his lodge. It might, for instance, refuse to restore his membership on the ground that exclusion from his lodge is an appropriate punishment; but where the decision of the lodge as to the guilt of the individual is reversed, and the Grand Lodge declares him to be innocent, or that the charge against him has not been proved, then I hold, that it is compelled by a just regard to the rights of the expelled member to restore him not only to the rights and privileges of Masonry, but also to membership in his lodge.

I cannot conceive how a Brother, whose innocence has been declared by the verdict of his Grand Lodge, can be deprived of his vested rights as the member of a particular lodge, without a violation of the principles of justice. If guilty, let his expulsion stand; but, if innocent, let him be placed in the same position in which he was before the passage of the unjust sentence of the lodge which has been reversed.

The whole error, for such I conceive it to be, in relation to this question of restoration to membership, arises, I suppose, from a misapprehension of an ancient regulation, which says that "no man can be entered a Brother in any particular lodge, or admitted a member thereof, without the unanimous consent of all the members"--which inherent privilege is said not to be subject to dispensation, "lest a turbulent member should thus be imposed upon them, which might spoil their harmony, or hinder the freedom of their communication, or even break and disperse the Lodge." But it should be remembered that this regulation altogether refers to the admission of new members, and not to the restoration of old ones--to the granting of a favor which the candidate solicits, and which the lodge may or may not, in its own good pleasure, see fit to confer, and not to the resumption of a vested and already acquired right, which, if it be a right, no lodge can withhold. The practical working of this system of incomplete restoration, in a by no means extreme case, will readily show its absurdity and injustice. A member having appealed from expulsion by his lodge to the Grand Lodge, that body calmly and fairly investigates the case. It finds that the appellant has been falsely accused of an offense which he has never committed; that he has been unfairly tried, and unjustly convicted. It declares him innocent--clearly and undoubtedly innocent, and far freer from any sort of condemnation than the prejudiced jurors who convicted him. Under these circumstances, it becomes obligatory that the Grand Lodge should restore him to the place he formerly occupied, and reinvest him with the rights of which he has been unjustly despoiled. But that it cannot do. It may restore him to the privileges of Masonry in general; but, innocent though he be, the Grand Lodge, in deference to the prejudices of his Brethren, must perpetuate a wrong, and punish this innocent person by expulsion from his lodge. I cannot, I dare not, while I remember the eternal principles of justice, subscribe to so monstrous an exercise of wrong--so flagrant an outrage upon private rights.

THE END

www.ingramcontent.com/pod-product-compliance
Lightning Source LLC
Chambersburg PA
CBHW080726020726
47503CB00010B/2808